MW01064500

Chasing Authenticity

SOLANGE JAZAYERI

FOUNDER OF MOMMYCEO.COM

LEADERS IN GLOBAL PUBLISHING

Published by True North Publishing
7777 N Wickham Rd, # 12-247
Melbourne, FL 32940
www.truenorthpub.com

Copyright 2015 © Solange Jazayeri
All Rights Reserved

No part of this book may be reproduced or transmitted in any form by any means: graphic, electronic, or mechanical, including photocopying, recording, taping or by any information storage or retrieval system without permission, in writing, from the authors, except for the inclusion of brief quotations in a review, article, book, or academic paper. The authors and publisher of this book and the associated materials have used their best efforts in preparing this material. The authors and publisher make no representations or warranties with respect to accuracy, applicability, fitness or completeness of the contents of this material. They disclaim any warranties expressed or implied, merchantability, or fitness for any particular purpose. The authors and publisher shall in no event be held liable for any loss or other damages, including but not limited to special, incidental, consequential, or other damages. If you have any questions or concerns, the advice of a competent professional should be sought.

Manufactured in the United States of America.

ISBN: 978-1-62865-144-7

Contents

G-D

Before there was Light, there was God. For this reason, my first expression of gratitude is directed towards the Creator. I was raised to call the Universe, our Higher Power, All That Is & Will Be, by the name God. As you read on, you will notice from this point forward I refer to this omniscient power as G-d. This is not out of disrespect. On the contrary, the primary reason for this spelling is to illustrate my respect, humility, and immense reverence towards this awesome force of Nature that is too vast and too expansive to be condensed inside three letters.

We are all evolving together. This book reflects who I am today. Perhaps with time, I will carry different, even opposing perspectives. Today, however, these words are what I believe to be true. What I know for sure is this: only Love is real. Loving yourself is G-ds highest order for us. For in loving ourselves we love G-d and all that is of this Universe.

Acknowledgements

I want to thank you, the reader. Without your eyes my message would only extend as far as my voice. You have given me the opportunity to extend it passed my life. As you hold space to read these pages, please know this book took two years to make, so that you and I would begin a conversation at this moment in time. I wrote this to integrate your soul's yearning to everyday living so you may teach others to do the same. There are ideas and concepts you may not agree with, or points you can expand and make better. I implore you to extend this conversation outward. What you don't agree with, I hope has helped you define more accurately and more strongly what you do believe. The ideas you can take to the next level, please do. The world needs your voice and your message. This is the significance behind Chasing Authenticity.

Writing a book is incredibly difficult on family and friends. As I faced the research and myself each morning my loved ones had to contend with me. It was not always pretty. Yet, my beautiful tribe found the heart to love me through it.

My name is listed as the author. It's a shame, really. Chasing Authenticity is not any more mine, than the perspectives I have gained from others are theirs. It is impossible to include all the names of those who have been of influence and who have been kind enough to help; for this, please forgive me. This body of work is an extension of the knowledge we all have gained from one another. There are family stories inside this book, but there are also insights I attained by passersby. There are teachers, poets, friendly strangers, and acquaintances who inspired me with one gesture or conversation or insight who I never again met. From the bottom of my heart, thank you.

There were groups of people that were particularly instrumental in the development of this book:

Don Osmond, thank you for investing in me. As we move forward in this new adventure I thank G-d you chose to hold my hand and help lead the way. You are a true blessing and an answer to my prayers.

Tucker Max, you took the time to say some hard truths. Your candidness and care replayed in my head over and over again urging me to dig deeper and look closer. Ryan Deiss and Perry Belcher, you two are a marketing powerhouse and I thank you for opening up a platform for authors like myself. Jennifer Rodriguez and Lindsay Marder, thank you for taking the project on. Juggling it all is a hard task and I appreciate your part in this book coming to life. I know your futures are bright and you will go far. Justin Sachs at Motivational Press delivered this book to readers. Thank you Justin, and your team for the commitment you show authors to help make their dreams possible.

The relationship between an editor and an author is special. There is a bartering dance that happens between words and ideas. I was lucky enough to work with three great editors (all with their own unique style & insight): Emil Prelic, Saundra Halgrimson, and Lindsay Marder. Emil was the first to introduce me to the boxing ring of writing. Thank you Emil for your boot camp training!! It was hardcore, but well worth the punches in strengthening up my style. Thank you for believing I was strong enough to take it. Behind that tough guy exterior is a man I respect and call a friend.

Saundra Halgrimson, for a year and half we nurtured the spirit of this book's message. You mentored me with an open heart and a compassionate ear. You are a badass, kind, generous, amazingly bright, and shiny woman. I love you Lady Bug! Every single cell in my body bows to your brilliance.

Everybody should have a work wife or work husband who will help pull you out of self-centeredness and speak to you candidly. Jared was my work husband. Jared, you encouraged and challenged me with your discernment and perspectives. I treasure our debates and thank you for sticking by me even when I drove you crazy. You are an amazing artist.

Carolina, my baby sister, you offered your help when I was at the midst of giving up. Muñeca, I am so in awe of you. Sprinkled in all these pages is your work and your love. Your support and commitment to this project was an act of love. Thank you for not allowing me to give up. Despite our eleven-year difference I believe laid on our hearts is the same mission to share and teach love and personal acceptance. Now this book is something that binds us even further together.

Sharing your final manuscript for the first time is an act of courage. Thank you Stephanie Lankowski for taking notes, opening a deeper dialogue, and writing uplifting words in that final draft. I hope your grace comes back to you infinity fold. You gave your time and help without asking for anything in return and for this gift I am eternally grateful.

Judging a book by its cover is more than an adage, it's a warning. I am appreciative to all the artists who shaped the first impression of Chasing Authenticity's message. Please forgive me as I insert some shameless plugs in this page, but it is the only way I know how to show tribute to all the wonderful artists who shared their talent with me. Art is to be shared and if you are moved by any of the artistry you have seen inside this book please feast your eyes on more as you visit their sites: Chrissy & Shane Sauers, thank you for taking the time to be my creative directors in the earliest days of my crafting a vision for Mommy, CEO and what Chasing Authenticity has now grown to become. I will always remember you scrambling to have me with a deadline of yesterday and coming through http://www.thoughtfactoryfilms.com. Hannah Bryant's portraiture of me is a true work of art. Hannah is a dear dear friend of mine, who has captured me on film for years. Thank you Hannah for bringing my soul's spirit to life in this front cover http://www.hbbphotography.com. Back cover photography credit goes to Marguerite Sadler. Thank you Mars for being so kind to open your lens and heart to me. Digital designer, Kate Herr was patient enough to work through several mockups until we got our book's signature just right. Thank you Ze design group! http://zedesigngroup.com. Laura's typography, Laura's typography titles our book at http://lauraworthington.com. Thank you for sharing your talent with the world.

It must be noted that there were advisor friends who squeezed in the time in their busy schedules to share with me their perspectives through their artistic eye. I am so thankful to my friends Jake Meyer at http://www.iwdff.com, and Kelly Housholder at http://fromscratchdesign.com who were honest and generous with their counsel.

Friendships are the family we chose and who chose us in return. Old friends who have chosen to stick by you become the signposts to your future accomplishments. Susan, three years ago you gifted me, *An Invisible Thread.* Inside the book this is what you wrote: *"Enjoy the book, and start outlining a book of your own!!!"* I took your advice. Thank you for being my cheerleader since seventh grade. You make everyone feel like they are your best friend. I am lucky to call you mine. Giselle, you and I grew up together. You are family to me. From undergrad to motherhood you have given me unconditional love. I am so proud of who we became together side-by-side. Your beauty which is striking (just take the compliment) pales in comparison to your compassion and care for others.

Most of these chapters were written because of key conversations I had with my friends. For this reason, I thank the following friends who each found their mark inside these pages. Katie, every time I think of you I smile. You are an example of wholeheartedness. Camy, thank you for sitting through my every heartbreak before my finding Nick. Our philosophical talks began my journey into a path of self-discovery. Sammy Hope, you are an amazing, true, and loyal friend. Thank you for loving me as I am and always holding space for our friendship. Naomi, ours is a spiritual friendship, timeless and precious. You planted the seeds of G-d's grace in me long ago. Cher, I owe my marriage and now my little girls to your counsel and care. Through Cherapy, I grew to understand the meaning and necessity of learning to love myself unconditionally. Because of your teaching of self-compassion I am a better wife and mother. Deb Doyle, you are a true guide, mentor, and friend. You are what a *strong successful and independent woman* should be defined as. Your integrity is admirable. I look to you as a reminder to always align character to vision. Jenny, thank you love for being you. Your devotion to G-d and His principles have been a source of strength to me. Your motivational words are always spoken with conviction and love. Kris and Sherry you were both my first true friends here in Destin. I remember having discussions with both of you of whether we should have children or not. Then whether we should have the second or not. So glad we did!!! I'm glad we took that leap of faith together. Kris, thank you for loving me at each stage of my life from *bringing the salad plate to picking up parenting books.* Our friendship is precious to me. Sherry and Daddy Warbucks, I love you both so very much. Nick and I have laughed with you for years and now our children will be raising the volume of our families' laughter. Jules, your friendship came to me as divine intervention. I am so grateful our children are best friends. The two of them model what embracing our beautiful differences can bring. Teadie, you give soul food a whole new meaning. Thank you for nourishing our bodies & spirit. Sarah Stone and Jennifer K. thank you for reading the earliest chapters of the book when they were virtually unreadable. More importantly, thank you for finding me when I had fallen off the face of this Earth. You two reminded me how important the balance of life and friendship is everyday. Jen you are the leader of our woman tribe and Sara you are an evolutionary woman. Mikka, thank for being the first to allow this book's message and opportunity to take flight. You are a beautiful soul I am so grateful I can witness you, Greta, and Joe come together. Jeremy, I wish you and Betheny a lifetime of happiness. In each other you have found a Love that is worth fighting for. May you be blessed as you bless those around you. Robin Wray, you once said to me we don't always get to see G-d's grace, but when we are lucky to get a glimpse of it, we are reminded of His perfection. His placing your home next to ours is just that—perfection. Susan Gogate, you are a miracle worker. In the short time we have met, you have had a huge impact on my life. True friendships are treasures because all there is as recompense is one another's presence.

To my teachers, I am grateful for the wisdom you have shared through friendship. Thank you Ms. Charlene and Ms. Flo for making the transition into pre-kindergarten so special. You will always hold a special place in my heart as you were the first to help my children understand Christ's love for us all.

Scott Martineau, your mentorship and your book, *The Power of You* got me through the darkest days of writing. Betty, in you I have witnessed what a life of devoting ourselves to our children can bring. Maryalice, you are one of the strongest women I know. Your work ethic and generosity is one I have always admired. My Dancing Lights, Debra, Deb, Ellen, Hope, and Amy. Our talks, laughter, and tears have been a gift to my soul. I am humbled to be among you in this pursuit of ours towards happiness. Tracy, thank you for inviting me to your book club and into your friendships with Celeste, Diane K, Diane T, Diane R and Barbara Luann. Being a part of women who gather around to talk about stories, life, and experiences in love through all its different angles has fed my mind and spirit in more ways than you will ever know. Eileen, part of this journey has come from your encouraging me to keep writing and believing in myself. I look back at past writings and I'm embarrassed, but still you showed me encouragement and I found courage. Prudence, thank you for introducing me to Transcendental meditation, the practice has been the catalyst for substantive change in my life. Coach Mary, as I hear you scream at our kids in the pool all summer long my body resonates with admiration. In my next lifetime, I wish to come back as you. You living out your passion and gift of teaching is a testimony to spiritual alignment.

Perhaps the most challenging aspect of writing this book was the time it took away from my beautiful sweet princesses. The only reason why I was even able to do it is because I trusted my support system. Chelsea, Melisse, Gertrudis, and of course Sara. Chels, I am so proud of what you have accomplished. To see you now, as both mother and teacher, fills my heart. Melisse, oh our beautiful Melisse! I am so glad you are the *cool teenager* the girls look up to. Gertru, you are a beautiful soul. Thank you for stepping in when I was sleep deprived to shower the girls with silly jokes and love. Sara, you more than anyone else understands how arduous this journey has been for me. How can I thank you for helping to mother my children, Nick and I? There are no words. All I can say is, G-d in his infinite wisdom paired us up together to show us both how loved we are.

Mr. and Mrs. Jazayeri, you have gifted me the sweetest most important gift of my life—your beautiful son—who has in turn, given me beautiful daughters. I am forever in your debt. My heart is filled with love and respect for you both.

Mama Dora, you are who first taught me to pray and love G-d. Your devotion has taught me we are never alone and His grace is always shining through us. Thank you for naming me Solange. I have tried my best to honor her name.

Cristina, you are who I share the most history with. Only you know me from early childhood. G-ds gift to allow me to be your sister is a true honor. You take care of us all in your own special way and we are all so grateful to you. Enrique, thank you for always bringing laughter. You too, like Cris, are an inspiration. Not many people have the stamina you have to make such a full life possible. Christian, you will always be our golden boy. I love you, love you, love you.

Papa, you've demonstrated the value of perseverance. This book is a tribute to those late nights and early mornings I saw you work through to provide for our family and us, your girls, more opportunities in the future.

Mama, here is another accomplishment you made possible for me. You taught me to dream big "because you can dream for free." I am lucky to have a mother who honors the importance of having your feet on the ground but your eyes towards the sky. Thank you for allowing me to find the strength within to go after my dreams and ambitions.

My last thank yous go to my home. Isadora and Nazareen, the day I realized I could write a book to memorialize my voice so I may always be within reach to guiding you with my humble advice, I knew it would be worth our family's sacrifice. This book was written with your future in mind. May you grow to be strong, kind, compassionate women. I know this will happen because you are both already strong, kind, and compassionate girls. I love you with every cell of my being and every breath of my spirit. I end by thanking my lover, Nick. Rasht, you are my best friend, my guide. Thank you for loving me. Thank you for building a life with me. And thank you, infinitely, for being the instrument who allows me to know unconditional love.

Dedication

To my mother, Celinda the original Mommy, CEO.

Within my soul is the knowing that we are all connected. In learning to accept and love ourselves more intimately, we grow to appreciate humankind. I am here, transparent before you, hoping my struggles may find a companion on this journey towards finding true self-worth.

Preface

I get why men like fast cars. I felt like a badass driving a super charged Mini Cooper. My life was a sort of Indie 500 race back then. Buying this car meant I'd arrived to a stadium of elite racers who chased after money and accolades at full speed. There was a preordained track I drove around in as fast as possible. First stop, college. Second, career. Third, house. Fourth, husband. Fifth stop, babies—maybe.

The faster the chase, the quicker the rewards and the happier I would be...or so I thought.

Making money was at the center of everything.

Paying for that Mini Cooper in full, just two years after opening my beauty laser business, made me feel as though I'd won the race. With check in hand, I walked into the car dealership to receive this hot rod as a trophy. My husband stood by my side. (Even though I would be paying for the car myself, back up was in order.) I was proud of myself, annoyingly proud, gloating actually at having this status symbol. This represented all my hard work and dedication. I can still relive the feelings of that day.

I can also recall the rage I felt when the car salesman looked straight at my husband, shook his hand, and began his sales pitch. His underlying assumption was obvious; Nick was buying the car for his 'pretty little lady.' Had the salesman with his good ol' boy charm shaken my hand at that moment, it would have charred his. But, he didn't. In fact, I'm not sure he saw me at all. Like a toddler, I angled my head back to observe the conversation taking place. Nick is about eight inches taller than I, but that day David and Goliath seemed more of a match than we did.

I've never felt so tiny, so miniature, and so miniscule. Looking back, it did me good. I had given the car salesman authority to measure my significance. I allowed his assumption to devalue my pride. Empowerment is the satisfaction we receive from ourselves when we recognize our potential and go after our dreams. Sore from the kick to the imaginary balls, my ego learned its lesson: we are who give others permission to disempower us. When we humble ourselves and put aside the trophies the true winnings come from our own personal integrity.

His lack of attention was not what had offended me; my own self-talk is what had led me astray. I thought chasing hard work and money would buy me the status of financially successful men. Chasing after external proof of our self-worth however, derails us from feeling the pleasure of self-respect and our authenticity.

Deeper introspection with this inner voice pointed to a deeper truth; the work itself, the influence of the service I was able to provide my clinic's patients, and ultimately the security and self-esteem that came from the commitment and opportunity to do meaningful work, was what was valuable, not the car nor the check. No one can buy or take away the self-respect that comes from applying our core principles into our work. Only I could measure this.

Had he practiced good salesmanship, he would have placed equal attention to us both, treating the sale as a joint decision. Whether paid for by my paycheck or not, women are decision makers, too. (Ever heard the saying "Happy wife, happy life"? Apparently, he had not.)

Honestly, quantifying self-worth by handing someone a check misses the mark.

It is normal for us to try to understand more of ourselves through the perception people have of us. That stranger represented a projection of what I perceived the world would see in me, a self-sufficient woman. However, basing my specialness on the judgment or lack of attention of others is illusionary.

In reality, for the most part, people we come across in our day-to-day actions, base thoughts of who we are on a single categorical interaction. This is called the Fundamental Attribution Error.

We assign an action to describe a personality rather than viewing someone inside the circumstance. The inappropriate salesmanship rustled up my sensitivities and I, in turn, minimized him by typecasting him as a chauvinist. Like him, I too made assumptions based on a short, fragmented interaction. It's typical for men to make the car-related decisions in a family. He probably based his assumption on past sales history. On the other hand, my prejudice came from the chip on the shoulder I carried around. I made his misstep personal. It's never personal. His lack of etiquette says more about him and his experiences with women, than it does about me. Our spending is a symbol of power that only shows off what we can afford, nothing more. We are *more than enough* just walking down the street being ourselves.

I used to think I didn't need a man. I chased them away to feel better about myself by feeling better than them. This inadequacy only left me feeling lonely. The funny part of this whole Mini Cooper story is that as much as I thought buying my own car proved I didn't need a man; I did need my husband at least to drive the car off the parking lot..

I didn't know how to drive a stick shift. Yes, I bought a car I could not even drive. Can you just imagine what that scene would have been like if I had made a big stink about being labeled a 'little lady' to only get in the car and have it put-put and stall as I tried to dramatically drive off?!

Introduction

To empower a woman is to inspire a family, a community, and ultimately humanity, for the journey of one woman is the plight of every woman and child. Like tunnels connecting the past to the future, each generation helps form the mindset of the next. Each of us must accept this responsibility in moving humankind forward.

The pill was immeasurably important to women because it unearthed a newfound freedom. Young, would-be mothers now had a fighting chance at becoming business leaders and winning autonomy, which had until then been reserved exclusively for men. Given men's inability to bear children, they were able to continue on a career path without physical interruption.

Eve's new apple, this tiny pill, awakened women both sexually and psychologically. There was a revolution, but with revolution, there's also pushback, so a time for adjustment has been taking place—an ebb and flow of negotiating new roles and responsibilities. Holding the power of fertility in the palm of our hands birthed the autonomous American woman—not only independent from men, but from the credo that we were made exclusively for the service of others. Our mentors told us we could do it all and, unfortunately, we internalized that to mean we must *be* it all.

Motherhood influences the emerging consciousness of another human being, but mothers or not, we're all interlinked as friends and neighbors—we're all caregivers to one another (not just women, but men, too). Humanity is both a verb and a noun, and we're its representatives. Having mothers who used their super powers for the higher good of our generation has made of us *Chasers,* a new iteration of wonder women, the archetypes we both wanted to emulate and feared becoming. With opportunities our mothers only dreamed of, we fumble with their torch and fall prey to their cautionary tale. Exhausted, we relive the sacrifice of flying high and fast, and being it all for everyone. It's costing us being ourselves. Constantly trying to outdo other Chasers for a first-place ribbon, we are left feeling sub-par with a great need to prove our worth. The worst part is that we're not outrunning anyone but ourselves...and we're burning out.

We've gotten it wrong. We substantiate who we are by what we *do,* instead of having what we do substantiate who we *are.* Each generation brings with it the social pressure of the last and with it, the variations we, as a whole, carve out for ourselves to make both our adolescence and adulthood distinctly ours. We've learned a lot, and taken much for granted from generations past. We're financially successful, but psychologically alone, unable to connect to what matters most—our individuality.

We stare with great intent at the bright future ahead, without recognizing the ground we're standing on now. Somewhere deep inside, we know we're chasing much more than applause and reputation; we're chasing a dream for something better, something more meaningful. The time for a more mindful movement has arrived. It begins with each one of us—it begins with you. It begins with the uncovering of an 'authentic self,' the inner being that strives to become self-actualized by experiencing our full potential—not only for ourselves, but also for our collective wisdom.

Satisfaction isn't intrinsic; it's our human struggle. To achieve more, we resist stagnation. Women's identity—our wants and needs—have evolved alongside our intellectual growth. Genetically hardwired to cross new frontiers as our physical needs are met, we reach out for our wants, and when achieving our wants, we still reach out for more. This reaching out has fueled the economics of our nation. Success and satisfaction have very different meanings when we begin to define them across age, gender, race, and social class. However, the most successful people don't let the box of society dictate how they go about their lives; they're happy not with what they have, but with how little they need.

Between mind-numbing work and play, Chasers are awakening. Our self-awareness has popped the blown up egos behind our paper maché personalities and a new shift in consciousness is underway. We are filling our personalities with something more substantial—a solid core of authenticity.

Not everything of value is quantifiable. Love and happiness are immeasurable. Therefore, the contents of this book had to pass a litmus test to help explain the following two questions:

1. Why don't we feel good enough despite all we have and all we are?

2. What mindsets help connect us to a more authentic self?

To be a positive influence we must become self-aware. The more we practice and protect our self-integrity, the better we become at understanding the inner struggles of others. There always will be someone able to outsmart and outrun us, but there also are those we can help. Our everyday choices matter, from the values we teach our children, to what we buy and consequently endorse. How we speak and behave towards one another matters. It all matters.

Our interactions with humanity, intricately interwoven, create in us a microcosm of the world. Male and female mindsets have distinct differences between decades, culture, and class. In addition, our definition of success differs from person to person. My own ethnicity as a first generation American with Latin-American parents has given me insight to these differences among cultural lines, the simple life juxtaposing a rags-to-riches dream that keeps Americans striving for more. The privileged and the poor have very different realities. The fact is, we are not all created equal or treated as equals. Ignoring our inequality has led our culture and our family structure astray. Everywhere we look, there is a hierarchy, as prevalent today as it ever was, and the responsibility of our lives rests within these realities.

Our Western culture reveres the best and brightest; being good enough is never *enough* unless we're *better than* someone else is. In trying to meet and exceed the standard, a battle ensues, the rivaling dialogues and messages of who we ought to be vs. who we truly are. Our greatest source of agitation is the catfight we've internalized of super-moms, sexy bunnies, Namaste yogis, and thirty-something careerists into our own posse of inner critics. Their incessant scrutinizing of our imperfections silences, or at best muffles, our inner voice and authenticity. In the words of poet and humanitarian Maya Angelou, "When we know better, we do better." Measuring ourselves against ideals misguides us and prevents us from knowing ourselves more fully.

We are the evolutionary product of our past, both physically and intellectually, and we're still evolving. We are competitive AND cooperative. We are individuals AND partners. We are daughters AND mothers AND friends AND lovers. We're all these things and not a single one. So, too, are the elements of our selfhood. We are our biology AND our psychology AND the force which allows us to change these elements. By learning how our biochemistry works and taking control of our own actions, thoughts, and feelings, we uncover the creative force within. A deeper understanding of our individual natures, heightens the understanding of the collective nature of (wo)mankind.

Our challenge now is to carve out an authentic self, and to get to know ourselves more deeply by practicing integrity. By not shying away from our imperfections or our gifts, we give others permission to do the same; if each of us speak truthfully about who we are, we're better able to tackle the human struggle together.

How to read this book

Many of us Chasers have tried our hardest to find self-validation in perfection. We believe self-reliance, financial success, and happy friends and family will bring us peace of mind and heart. However, in our need to be it all for everyone, we have lost pieces of our authenticity and self-worth.

To understand what formulates our self-concept, *Chasing Authenticity* fragments the elements of self-criticism and builds on that exploration. It underscores the idea that humans perceive stimuli in two different ways: either by instinct or mindful consciousness. We are complex beings with complicated emotions. To understand others better, we must accept our own duality and evolve from it. Our instincts are patterns of behavior and thought that have become habitual reactions. Mindful consciousness, on the other hand, has us take a moment to choose perspective and action to a given situation. Rather than chasing after ideals, we discuss how to uncover personal integrity and make mindful living (and thinking) a daily practice.

Three major milestones form our identity and self-concept as adults. The first is our inherited self, formed from our family of origin. As we mature, we seek individuation. At this second stage, we form an identity separate from our family. Finally, the third stage brings us back into dependent relationships.

As we fall in love, we negotiate who we are once more. Trusting our partners, but more importantly trusting we are enough as we are, is what allows us to build intimacy. Love, therefore, is the key message in this book. Love for ourselves, love for each other, and love for humanity. The discipline of self-compassion is a practice in inner-validation. We really can stop chasing something outside our grasp and find the courage to live an authentic life.

Concluding with a personality survey, you may uncover what your neuro-chemistry defines as your core values.

Inherited Self

Chapter 1: Our Time is Now...

Chapter One lays the foundation for our work. In this chapter, we consider how our brain chemistry, family values, and culture affect the adult choices of career and family. More importantly, we begin examining why we have abandoned what we love so we can reconnect to that which enlivens us.

Chapter 2: Mirror, Mirror...Who Is The Fairest of Us All?

That which receives our attention shapes our mind. In this chapter, we pull the curtain back on why media has packaged and branded judgment as a marketable product. The effects of Reality TV and Celebritism have been so effective in captivating our senses that we are becoming more critical towards others, and inevitably more critical of ourselves. Understanding the seduction of neuro-marketing empowers us to make more conscientious choices.

Chapter 3: Hippity-Hop...

Our sexual identity helps determine how we give and accept love. The glamorization of pornography has made adult stars real competitors inside our bedrooms. Chapter Three explains the difference between fantasy and play, and how authenticity heightens our sexual expression to honor your sensuality.

Chapter 4: It's Just Business...

We discuss the business of making babies. Children challenge our personal choices both financially and biologically. As our economy has forced us to bring work to our families, our next political frontier is to bring families to work. Chapter Four teaches how your vote and your voice impacts the opportunities we as women receive.

Chapter 5: Eve's New Apple...

Why do we compare, contrast, and compete against other women? The objective of this chapter is to have us embrace the different choices women make. In respecting the different choices of others, we learn to appreciate the competing identities inside ourselves so we may better practice self-compassion.

Self-Integrity
Chapter 6: Being Discovered...

We revisit our personality styles and the words and labels that are particularly instrumental in our self-talk (negative or otherwise). This is where we define our distinct core values. After looking at how the external world influences our personalities, now we take a closer more intimate view as to how these topics affect our intimate relationships.

Chapter 7: Imperfections...

This chapter explains how Chaser's type E* personality (wanting to be everything to everybody) is driving the integrity of our relationships down. **Imperfections** offers a four step practice to quieting down the 'not good enough' speak of our inner critics.

Chapter 8: Perfect Measurements...

Food is at the cornerstone of our everyday living. In this chapter, we connect health and fitness to a practice of self-care. Instead of beating ourselves up for every morsel of food we ingest, this section urges you to make a healthy lifestyle a practice of self-compassion.

Chapter 9: Removing the Mask ...

Although it has become harder and harder for us to trust in marriage and love ever lasting, having faith in one another evolves us personally. This chapter illustrates how learning to be vulnerable & trust increases emotional intimacy and long lasting relationships.

Trusting the Tribe
Chapter 10: Trust and the Tribe...

We come back full circle as our journey reaches its end. This chapter teaches us how to accept that we can't do it all on our own. We need a community of supporters to evolve personally and in our relationships, to be emotionally successful.

Chapter 11: Chasing the Illusion...

This book would not be complete if we did not acknowledge that there exists a Higher Power & Purpose in us all. ***Chasing the Illusion*** has us take a leap of faith so we may become self-actualized from the sense of humanity and Oneness that resides within us.

Chapter 12: Mommy CEO...

This chapter concludes our time together. I offer my invitation to step into your present and explore, discover, and evolve together as we create a community dedicated to celebrating what it means to walk in our authenticity.

To get a more personalized experience as you read ***Chasing Authenticity,*** consider Dr. Helen Fisher's research on what makes up your personality style. An evolutionary psychologist and researcher, Fisher contends there are four chemicals that affect our temperaments, which can decode why we love what we love. To find your style, take Fisher's quiz by visiting http://www.chemistry.com

It is my theory, that these chemicals and personality styles birth our inner critics. The four personality styles Helen Fisher profiles with their associated neuro-chemical are as follows:

Explorers (who I refer to as Ms. Wonder)

Driven by dopamine and the related norepinephrine system, and greatly motivated by novelty, explorers are sensation seeking individuals who find enjoyment in the thrill of the chase, whether it be knowledge or adventure. Goal-oriented and assertive, Explorers have big wins because of their ability to gamble high. They are the open-minded pioneers of the world who march to the beat of their own drum, understanding there's an exchange between adventure and the comfort of safety. Explorers are optimistic, but they're also likely to get bored easily if not engaged in a high degree of creativity.

Builders (who I later refer to as Ms. Rosie)

Driven by serotonin and loyal protectors who want to belong to a community, Builders are those we trust to schedule events. They pay attention to detail and are very orderly, step-by-step linear thinkers. Oftentimes religious or faithful in their spiritual practice, these individuals have high moral standards and respect the good of the whole. Builders are disciplined but, at times, inflexible in their ability to accept the unconventional.

Negotiators (who I later refer to as Ms. Homemaker)

Driven by estrogen and the oxytocin system, negotiators are humanitarians. They're the most willing to make personal concessions to make others happy. Their mental flexibility allows them to hold two opposing views as *different perspectives* rather than contradictory. These individuals are natural-born counselors and diplomats as they express more activity in the region of the brain associated with eempathy and are able to see themselves in others. Sociability and introspection is high on their list given their high emotional intelligence.

Directors (who I later refer to as Ms. Bossy)

Driven by testosterone and leading with logic (exclude any emotion) makes Directors frank, stoic heroes. They have narrowly focused, but intense interests. They're prone to quick, decisive action. Autonomy, independence, and success are of high interests to this temperament. They appreciate rank as they take responsibility for the care of their duties. Directors are *systematic*, focusing on the problem at hand without outside noise. Strategic intelligence is their strength.

Kaleidoscope

The phases of women are
those of kaleidoscopes.
Life dials new dimensions,
to reveal mosaics of color and light;
Connecting, evolving, morphing reincarnations.
Each collage—a tribute
to who they love, have loved, will love.

Love what you see in each rotation.
For it isn't in the colors you exist.
You are not one color.

Your intricate design
is our Soul's radiance
illuminating the prism of your body
so Love can dance gallantly

Honor the translucence
of your color filled tiles,
It is here you exist.
Find yourself.
To dim your light, to not allow its abundant splendor,
robs the world of witnessing the full spectrum of who you are.
And who you are meant to inspire.

Chapter 1

Our Time is Now

"Get me some poets as managers. [Poets] contemplate the world in which we live and feel obligated to interpret and give expression to it in a way that makes the reader understand how that world runs. It is from their midst that I believe we will draw tomorrow's new business leaders."

Sidney Harman (Multi-millionaire businessman, publisher, and engineer)

*I*t's often said we cannot fall in love until we first love ourselves, yet it's precisely in understanding what we love that we realize our identity. Long before knowing who I was, I'd fallen helplessly and hopelessly in love countless of times: with poetry and fashion, with my husband and children, and the possible honor of achieving the badge of *Extraordinary*. The first love I ever had was an old, yellowing poetry book perfumed with the scent of dust and mildew. While others disregarded its value, it was a biblical treasure to me. Those musky, tethered, discolored sheets carried the secret language of artists, the essence of humanity. I can admit my attachment to this book was a bit obsessive, but overexcitement is forgiven in the young. Rehearsing poetry transformed my timidity to confidence. Just as peacocks spread their mantle, my ego unfolded like a Spanish fan in each recited composition.

As children, we learn how and what to love about ourselves from the self-concept our caregivers help us formulate. Although we authorize them to define our identity, allowing them to quantify what is meaningful, no outsider is capable of feeling our unique experiences and therefore able to truly assess what we want to experience most in ourselves. When the cute girly performances carried into my adolescence, adults reasoned I had *too much potential to waste* on romantic ventures. Poetry was termed *a poor man's game*, motivated by emotions, not promotions, and seriously lacking in ambition or drive. Therefore, the yellow poetry book was closed and put aside to collect dust once again. The definition of what potential actually meant remained unclear. No one really defined it. However, like Girl Scout badges, it seemed that making the most of one's potential meant having prestigious attachés like M.D., J.D., and the like.

As girls, we no longer limited our dolls to motherhood or traditional female roles. Although, we are not often explained what the 'pill' is, as children the assumption we will one day take such pill lies hidden behind two main questions: how many babies will we have and what do we want to become when we grow up. These are loaded questions, many times in opposition to one another. The pill unearthed a newfound freedom. Young, would-be mothers now have a fighting chance at becoming business leaders and winning the autonomy, which had, until the pill, been reserved exclusively for men. We too can now continue on a career path without physical interruption. The desire for higher paying careers has become more impressive to women, and motherhood now often times takes a back seat to personal and intellectual development to make room for career-driven ambitions. Yet, despite all our advancements, there has been a high price to pay in return; divorce has hit an all-time high, young marriages have plummeted to an all-time low, and economic security has become a very real necessity for women.

Validated Self-esteem vs. Self-respect

Our parents thought IQ and a high self-esteem would determine how well we performed later in life. Thus, praise, achievements, and high expectations grounded our self-concept. Everybody received a trophy. There were no losers, only winners. Coming up short of the best was not an option. Innate intelligence, awards, and honorary titles received the grand applause. Even rulebooks changed so we could have more wins and fewer losses. If ever failure seemed imminent, Band-Aids over our tender hearts kept the scabs of defeat from scarring our super-sized egos. As a result, we were sheltered from challenges that could possibly defame our genius. *Fear of failure* was the underlying message. However, basing our self-concept on innate talents can dispirit us when we face adversity (which our loving and good intentioned parents didn't know at the time) because focusing just on natural talents alone (rather than on core values) blocks the development of sheer grit.

The sparkling *You're Extra Special* badges, proudly worn, verified we were the best child. This unearned confidence and lack of honesty cut our endurance at the knees. True resilience faltered when our goals seemed too far out of reach. Our parents gifted us designer shades to prepare us for our entitled bright futures. However, adulthood brought us into the Great Recession and our sense of self stood on shaky ground as we tried to balance more than we could handle. Today we're older, but not so much wiser. Although there aren't paparazzi waiting outside our front door, we're the self-promoting and self-made celebrities of YouTube, Twitter, Facebook, and Instagram, displaying an entitled *all-about-me* attitude with incredibly high self-esteem and shockingly low self-awareness.

Contrary to the intuition of many, the best way to raise self-esteem and motivation is not by praising intelligence. World-renowned psychologist Carol Dweck, Ph.D. has built her career on studying the psychology of success. She found that building an identity around our fixed traits (i.e. inherent intelligence and talent) actually can jeopardize our self-worth and future achievements, ultimately preventing us from accepting the value of new challenges and personal evolution. In 1998, along with Claudia M. Mueller, Ph.D., Dweck conducted six studies to test the effects of praise on children and found that congratulating innate intelligence had a negative effect on motivation and overall self-perception.

According to the studies, the students praised for their intelligence did their best to protect this label. They became frustrated and disenfranchised with tests or puzzles they could not conquer (presumably second-guessing their smarts). Some even abandoned their activity before the threat to their praised intelligence became real. In contrast, those students praised for their ***effort*** felt stimulated by challenges, moreover, enthused by the exercise in perseverance. Our brains are hardwired for lifelong learning. What we focus on is what will determine our identities, intelligence, and quality of life. When Dweck taught individuals the growth mindset, centered on the value of practice in the development of the brain's learning, individuals were much more likely to persevere past their fear of failure.

The game of life is not just about showing up and pinning the class participation award. There's a difference between failing at something and being a failure. Failing is a privilege and a rite of passage. The ultimate reward is grit. To earn self-respect we must shake off defeat and use it as fuel to practice, practice, practice.

The scars of heartbreak toughen us up. It's the work, the struggle, and the commitment to prevailing over our self-limiting mindsets that make victory so sweet. We're all ordinary human beings ***capable*** of doing extraordinary things. New York Times Bestseller, Paul Tough, author of *How Children Succeed*, researched two opposing socio-economic scales and concluded character, how we process and overcome challenges, and failure through support networks and personal mindsets, is the key ingredient to well-being and future performance. Data indicates grit is irrelevant or at times, even inversely related to measurements of talent. Yet, grit is the most significant predictor of high performance (in life and in work). Many talented individuals lack follow-through and stamina. The *extra* in extraordinary comes from *perseverance*, not from social intelligence, physical beauty, or strength. The determination to overcome obstacles is what allows at-risk teens to thrive, sales people to keep their jobs in low economic times, and teachers to become exemplary.

Evolving Together

Good and bad advice is hard to discern when we do not yet have a concrete sense of self. Despite a relatively new understanding of our evaluation of time and money, society still warns us that we must secure a certain level of financial success. We're told the more commas and zeroes in a paycheck, the happier we will be. Creative elective courses that help our soul evolve are under-funded. Conventional classes like Economics are what are held in high esteem. Consequently scholastic careers, vocation, and mindsets follow that evaluation system. The System has children as young as twelve years old making life decisions as to whether they want to get on a medical or engineering professional track, before they're even able to ascertain their identity, let alone comprehend who they will be and what will be most meaningful in adulthood. There's an ever-increasing pressure in schools to stay ahead of the curve intellectually. However, our emotional and personal development curve is what determines the richness of our daily life.

An overindulgent self-esteem manifested in us, based on two influential reports in the mid 1990s, which changed school programs and consequently our self-concept. The first, by The Carnegie Corporation, forewarned parents the first three years of life were critical to learning. With the decline of cognitive skills in America, children were entering kindergarten ill prepared. Both academic institutions and families were directed to 'up the ante.' The second, *The Bell Curve* by Charles Murray and Richard Herrnstein, evidenced Intelligence Quotient (IQ) to be the most influential predictor of future success. The cognitive hypothesis therefore became the foundation of teaching: curriculums sharpened the skills measured by IQ tests, through practice, repetition, and early exposure.

The effects of these cautionary tales have been long lasting. Programs such as *Baby Can Read* and *Baby Einstein*, created for infant learning and development are popular products today—capitalizing on the notion that early exposure raises IQ. Confession: I, too, rush to stores to buy *learn by play* tools for my daughters. However, the implicit message here (let's face it) is *learn more than you play!* We now expect our five-year-old children to read upon Kindergarten graduation and twelve-year-old students in metropolitan areas are increasingly pressured to choose scholastic tracks to be more competitive upon entering high school. The social pressure for professional training is so overwhelming in youth that children's innate desire to live in the moment, to experience fun, creativity, and joy (qualities that help us know ourselves more deeply) are re-categorized as a waste of time. Perhaps after retirement, we will give ourselves permission to have the unabated fun we let go of in our youth or finally compose poems we never had the time to write....right?

Our parents did the best with what they knew, but today we know better. Every decade and every generation brings new waves of social consciousness. We're evolving together. Believing that we're only as smart as our GMAT and LSAT scores makes us obvious targets to over-stressing our own children in early scholastic development programs. There is value to these programs, of course, but if we can't laugh and play as children, when can we? An excessive focus on cognitive skills and development without a balanced amount of R&R is responsible for building the seemingly celebrated mindset that what we have, and how much trivia we know, equates to who we are.

Roman's Story

On a car ride to work, Giselle, my best friend, saw her son withdraw from their conversation and become pensive. As they drove past a poor neighborhood, Roman seemed disturbed by the disparity in landscape. They crossed over the street boundary socially marked the 'right' and 'wrong' side of town. Roman began asking why the houses were so big and nice on one side and not on the other. Giselle explained that the families in the nicer neighborhoods had higher paying careers, therefore able to afford the manicured yards, cleanliness, and safety.

When he was then asked, "What do you want to be when you grow up?" Roman contemplated the different professions of his parents. Giselle held a high-ranking position in a long-term care facility for children and his father was a well-accomplished engineer. Perhaps it was their lack of more heroic job titles, such as president and firefighter, which caused Roman's long pause. From the back of the car, propped up by his booster seat, he looked straight at the rearview mirror into his mother's eyes and decisively answered, "G-d."

Giselle: "What!? No, Roman, I'm sorry, but you can't be G-d!"

Roman: "Why not? You said I could be whatever I wanted to be and I want to be G-d."

It is hard to argue his case. Biting her lip from laughing, Giselle then asked (hoping to match a profession to the god-like qualities Roman sought) what part of G-d's profession he wanted to embody so she could offer some guidance. This was the moment she expected her sweet boy to say something altruistic and loving but instead he responded with, "G-d is the boss of the world and I want to be the boss of everyone."

There's a difference between healthy self-esteem and delusion. Roman's parents named Roman after the Roman Empire because they wanted him to be strong and courageous, characteristics much needed in order to reach our fullest potential. We need courage to overcome our insufficiencies and fully accept the breadth of our tremendous capabilities. Strength allows us to get up again and again from the letdowns of life. However, these qualities are values that require persistent practice. Courage does not exist without fear, and attaining strength is not viable without fortifying our resilience and pushing past our comfort zones. Resilience ushers in the life we are intended to live. That authentic life first shows itself in our imagination, it tests our beliefs, and as those beliefs mature, they develop into inner wisdom. Roman's imagination allowed him to contemplate becoming G-d. Personal evolution teaches us our beliefs don't always match reality and in our negotiation between our beliefs and limitations, we often find our more authentic selves.

Inner wisdom can only grow through personal experience (aka mistakes, wrong turns, and sometimes, poor choices). Certainly, we want our children to see themselves in the best possible light so they may embrace their inner being, which houses Godlike unconditional love. Self-actualization connects us to humanity or the G-d within us. However, most would agree that believing they are *G-d, bosses of everything* ,is a contradiction to compassionate god-like love. All jokes aside, a sense of grandiosity and entitlement as a result of wanting to build healthy self-esteem is a concern for many parents. Healthy parenting balances self-esteem and authenticity so that a healthy self-concept is not based on falsehood, but by accepting our individuality and practicing our personal values day-in and day-out.

The tall, smart, and good-looking do not have reserved exclusivity for positive self-esteem. Confidence and self-worth exist on different planes, as does, conceitedness, which is an expression of low self-worth. Those who have a solid sense of self are kind to others. They are assertive, but not degrading. Positive self-perception requires encouragement so we may develop our natural gifts and affinities. Father of enlightened management, Abraham Maslow, would ask his students to think of whom they considered the next brilliant mind. Who among them believed themselves to be writing the greatest American novel? Who would be the most influential leader, political figure, or saint? Students would giggle and fidget in their seats. "If not you, then who?" The fear of appearing too grandiose or boastful can cast self-limiting shadows over our aims. Be assured dissatisfaction lies before us if we do not sum up the courage to honor our self-actualization.

In the words of Maslow, "We fear our highest possibilities (as well as our lowest ones). We're generally afraid to become that which we can glimpse in our most perfect moments, under the most perfect conditions, under conditions of great courage. We enjoy, and even thrill, to the god-like possibilities we see in ourselves in such peak moments. And yet, we simultaneously shiver with weakness, awe, and fear before those very same possibilities."

I've been fortunate to study under Tal Ben-Shahar stemmed from teaching the most popular course in H Positive Psychology on how to be happy. Despite his s introverted nature, he's an articulate, powerful, yet hu speaks frankly of his own struggles with self-esteem a and candidly shares the insights gained from his resea..... ɪaɪ ʙen-Shahar completed his dissertation in 2004 and titled his thesis *Restoring Self-esteem's Self-Esteem: Constructs of Dependent and Competence and Worth.* Perhaps the most illuminating aspect of his study is the correlation he found between happiness and a positive self-esteem. (The high correlation of .68 substantiated the relevance of our uncensored self-evaluation to our feeling of contentment.) Drawing from the philosophies of Maslow, Nathaniel Branden, and several other psychologists and researchers, Dr. Ben-Shahar argues that the development of self-esteem must shift from dependent to independent before reaching an unconditional phase. Dependent self-esteem necessitates the encouragement of others. Independent self-esteem speaks of inner motivation. When we are able to reach the unconditional level of self-esteem, we feel so integrated with an activity or a moment that a sense of self is lost as we become immersed in the experience.

The Value of Time and Money

In a way, we've lived for this very moment: the age in which we prove ourselves and demonstrate we *are* the extraordinary women society expected us to become. Our ethos growing up was we could be whatever we set our minds to be. In turn, we worked hard as girls and adolescents to *have it all* and become beautiful and rich. Nevertheless, when our looks, status, and money are gone, what we have left is our most basic self. After the negotiation of our likes and loves, (what we need vs. what we desire) is over, it is then we begin to craft our most authentic self; an identity based not on what we own, but what we value.

eri

though preparation is necessary, remaining true to an authentic lf is what guarantees inner peace. There will always be an internal conflict when we seek external validation. Society informs us of what is socially right and wrong, and slowly we find ourselves abandoning our natural affinities and bartering our most vital curiosities for the dreams others have for us. However, what our loved ones believe is best for us can lead us astray from our best self.

The minute we start making decisions about who we will be as adults, we begin negotiating who we are in the moment. It is in this negotiation of our interests, that we can differentiate what it is we view as transient love versus unconditional love. There are fleeting love affairs that awaken us, but don't stay forever. Then there are those loves we tirelessly defend (even committing our life to) so they may teach us about ourselves. To be sure, if becoming a famous world-class poet could have been guaranteed, no one would discourage this vocation. Unfortunately, there are no guarantees in life. Sometimes we need to choose what's safe so it affords us the opportunity to do or have what we most value and love. However, in abandoning our need to impress others, we begin to search for the genius, the inspiration within us. Making the courageous choice to integrate that, which enlivens us into each day, can bring a deep recompense.

We fear being unproductive, but boredom breeds ingenuity. Albert Einstein used to play the piano for hours when he was stuck on a complex theory so he could let go of his intellect and allow his genius to find him. As research dollars bridge scientific study into mainstream culture, behavioral economists, authors, and journalists, such as Daniel Pink and Malcolm Gladwell are changing the way we evaluate and choose our occupations. What feels most like success is being in a state of harmony with oneself emerging from inner creativity and flow. Experiencing a sense of our individuality within the work we choose provides more self-satisfaction than money and status alone. **Work that empowers us also liberates us and extends time by providing a higher degree of meaning.**

We first must identify what is most purposeful to us as individuals, in order for our work to energize us. Defining potential as the embodiment of exemplary daughters, one-day to be wives and mothers, has cemented us into a world dictated by our family and that of our *future family*. Perhaps this is why we are delaying our family planning just long enough to enjoy a space between these milestones.

It feels as though to have our romance or career reach its highest potential twenty-four hour care and devotion is required of us. Learning to balance love and life in the structure of our daily schedules is how we find ourselves. We need not lose ourselves in either work or family; we must instead find ourselves amongst them.

There's always been a race against time inside of me, a hostile pursuit towards having it all. To gain validation (by having achieved a certain measure of female empowerment), I went to business school and graduated with an MBA. Planned motherhood and workaholism was, or so I thought, the first natural step towards children. To allow myself the right to consider motherhood, a certain amount of financial success was imperative. Work faster, more diligently, more aggressively...more, more, more, faster, faster, faster! However, instead of finding validation, what I found was a contradiction. The fine print and subtext to the diploma read: *To ensure independence and self-reliance, we advise female professionals to ignore biological and psychological needs for financial gains.*

The problem with shortcuts and faster trains is that you miss a lot of scenery along the way. Sure, we get there faster, but it also makes for a much bumpier ride. Applied medicine warns that by our late twenties our fertility begins to decrease, and by age 35 the health risks for both mother and baby increase exponentially. This pressure led to a mid-life crisis on the eve of my twenty-fifth birthday.

"I'm going to have babies tomorrow and I have nothing to show for it."

Intuitively I knew that children would require I give up more of myself. Transforming that time-sensitive-fear into motivation, eight months after my midlife crisis the doors to my own laser aesthetics business opened. Within three years, Nick and I were married and that small business became my first baby. Unfortunately, I don't remember our first years of marriage because my workaholism lead to seven-day work weeks. Until my business became successful, my life was all business. I exchanged dinner parties for networking events. Whenever I did attend friends' cooking parties, the dish I always held was a salad: quick and easy. Likewise, these salads were a status symbol of my denial of anything feminine and domestic, and evidence I was too busy building up success to slow down and cook.

I once thought increasing wealth would increase self-worth. However, self-satisfaction just became more and more elusive. Once a goal had been met, there was another, far loftier goal to conquer. The only way to decompress at the end of the day was inside a glass of wine… sipping it down slowly so the day's work could melt away from my tense, stressed out shoulders. The sense of accomplishment felt good, but only temporarily. The more I worked, the more disconnected I became and the harder it got to relax and de-stress. Only wine helped me to just *be*. One day it became obvious that female empowerment did not equal female fulfillment.

Mihaly Csikszentmihalyi, a Positive Psychology Professor and Director of the Quality of Life Research Center, reports that regardless of culture or education, flow brings about clarity of mind where, even through difficult circumstances, the sense of time is suspended, and along with it goes our need to calibrate our level of happiness. We enter a state of *being* where the *self* disappears and becomes part of something greater. Contemplate this thought: if time is the one resource we cannot barter, then it goes to reason it's our most expensive commodity. We exchange money for expertise, creativity, and know-how, but in the end, what we try to do is compensate others for saving us time so we can allot more energy and attention to the people, things, or activities we love. Doing what we love enables us to feel more connected to our authentic self, more able to embrace inner peace and appreciate who we are in the here-and-now. So, what if we concentrate on developing self-integrity through choices that are more in line with our authentic self? Then will we grow to understand the value of time and money?

Seeking Validation in External Measures

Work has become a defining issue in women's lives. It puts our core values to the test and forces us to make decisions about where we expend our emotional and physical energy. Make living your life your vocation. Practice living in meditation by immersing yourself fully into each experience and the learning of each new thing. Written between the fifth to the second century BC, the Bhagavad-Gita is a 700-verse Hindu scripture found within the *Mahabharata*, the worlds longest poem, known as the remembered tradition and embedded within its verses is this truth: *we are entitled to our labor, not to the fruits of our labor.* By placing our evolutionary measure on titles, rank, and salaries, we miss the unveiling of our individuality inside the work itself. Money is a very real necessity when we're paying for healthcare, but when our mindset becomes trapped in the allure of luxury and status, money takes on a distorted reality. Salaries can never validate the worth of our life's vocation. The seed of our soul propagates (be it thought or artistry) in the mind of other human beings. Philosophers, poets, mothers, may not have lofty paychecks, but they do plant seeds of inspiration.

Each one of us is entitled to do what our soul yearns to do, and it is then that we feel satisfaction. Work should become a vehicle that validates our personal growth regardless of title or position. Although, there are a few people who simply are *money-rich* and *character-poor*. We can find happiness and inner peace in being satisfied with the integrity of our character. Inevitably, we come to recognize that we live our days longer than we do the individual phases of our life. For how quickly a lifetime transpires! Whatever is more precious than our limited allotted time? Cash money is not what we want most—but the freedom that it grants us to extend our life's experience is what we unconsciously seek. Perhaps in the future we'll look at our professions and careers in a different way, not just as a part of life, but a part of *our life* that helps us *feel* alive and helps us to extend the moments in which we felt most alive.

To embrace inner peace is to appreciate the here-and-now as ordinary people. Seek to connect to that which you enjoy. **Developing** integrity makes us elect growth choices that evolve from the traits we most love about ourselves. World-renowned anthropologist Helen Fisher is perhaps the foremost expert on the biology of our personalities. If there is such a thing as an intellectual crush, she's it for me! I'd be a groupie at her concert if the academic world had such a thing. When she paired up with Chemistry.com, they gave Fisher the opportunity to analyze the natural affinities and attraction of over half a million people around the globe to verify her hypothesis of how our chemistry affects our identities. Through the scanning of 45 people in an MRI brain scan, she found that there are biological reasons for our behavior.

She states, "...there are patterns to personality but there [is] no randomness, personality is not random as nature is not random."

The Phenomenal Four

Each personality type is important in its own way; after all, they have been responsible for moving civilization forward. Perhaps in the future, instead of evaluating IQs and earning potential we will evaluate the natural gifts our personality styles present within us, so we can bring who we are into our occupation. **Our core values are written in our biochemistry, if only we listen.**

When our brains form inside our mother's womb, each of us receives a unique cocktail of neurochemicals that affect our perceptions and relationships. As we all know, nurture plays an important, critical part in our psyche, but it's also true that our genetic coding intimately ties into our perspectives. Fisher makes it a point to clarify that these temperaments are not personality *types*, but *styles*. We have all four temperaments, yet most of us have a primary and secondary brain system that expresses it more acutely. Each temperament carries with it its own set of behavioral patterns and inclinations. Although there are myriad chemical and neural networks which help compose our personality styles, the four neural systems Fisher bases her research upon are: 1) dopamine and related norepinephrine system, 2) serotonin, 3) testosterone, and 4) estrogen and oxytocin system. To illustrate these styles, think of Wonder Woman's need for adventure. Those of us who appreciate living without restraint in order to feel enlivened by adventure and excitement are likely to have within them higher levels of dopamine. By contrast those who are more inclined to structure their life around ensuring the family's safety are examples of serotonin's Rosie Riveter; stable, uncompromising in their beliefs, and trustworthy. Testosterone driven individuals are associated with the Lady Boss stereotype because of their direct communication and hard driving work style, often for their commitment to rank and status. And to conclude, estrogen, the neurochemical expressed highest in women, can be personified by the Homemaker style who seeks to bring harmony and nurturing to those around us in their emotional and intuitive nature.

This theory helps explain why some of us are more open minded vs. judgmental, why it's easier for women to tap into empathetic areas of the brain, and why men typically are more valiant. To evaluate these styles, Fisher formulated the Fisher Temperament Inventory (FTI) questionnaire, which as of 2012, 10 million people have taken it (that's about 30,000 people weekly). To find your style, take Fisher's quiz by visiting http://www.chemistry.com.

CHAPTER 2

Mirror, Mirror...Who Is The Fairest of Us All?

"Once you make a declaration of who you are by choosing your core values, you begin to affirm your belief in who you are,"
Scott Martineau, *The Power Of You*

*O*ur modern-day feminine mystique, the creative force which attracts lovers and draws children to our care, lives in between our physiology and psychology, not between our independence and financial achievement. Nevertheless, our youth took place inside the greed-is-good era of the eighties and nineties, and although this brought America prosperity, that prosperity was temporary and the negative implications for humanity have been high. The now full-grown Trophy Kids have become a new segment for marketers to target, and they have readily seized that opportunity to restore our fairytale self-esteems, promising us another chance at Trophy Girls status. We can be the best **if only** we buy perfection...youth, glamour, and fame.

As media highlights our insecurities and fears, it drives us mindlessly to exchange our principles for external validation. Despite the 85% purchasing power women hold, we unwittingly continue to sanction sensationalism, sexism, and celebrity-ism with our dollars. This naïveté has cost young girls and women our self-respect. With the *Look-at-me, What-are-you-famous-for* culture, permission to attack women in media has reached a record high. Women and men are being socialized to criticize others with very limited information—a simple press of a button deems a person 'hot or not', friend or a foe nowadays. Celebrity-bashing blogs and Reality TV invites viewers to judge, stereotype, and caricaturize women, (specifically our body parts), reducing us to labels. An object to be judged, measured, and exploited. Please note, highlight, write down, and repeat aloud a hundred times, whatever you have to do, but remember this: **Reducing a human being to a thing or a label is the first step towards cruelty.**

I love beautiful things like art, clothes, models, etc., but as fashion and style shows have become personally attacking towards contestants, it's become harder and harder to appreciate beauty for beauty's sake. Judges now contend against one another to outdo the other's sarcasm. It's understood the panel has *cart blanche* to say whatever they want about contestants. Each show raises the bar of unkindness. In addition, we allow this defaming to occur because we idolize celebrities, not based on character strengths or compassion, but on notoriety. In your own life, if a contemptuous chef screamed obscenities at his staff, you would call him a jerk and get him fired. If a judge or a justice of the peace squawked at immature, sometimes unintelligent citizens with cruel words, you would question her credibility. Yet, we increasingly find ourselves TiVo'ing these shows, so we can watch them at another more convenient time...when we're relaxing!

What's relaxing about watching the exploitation of humanity for the sake of ratings? If you enjoy winding down by reading the latest tabloid, voting on who should make it to the next round on TV, and watching women become famous simply on what they own or what they look like, you're much more likely to gossip about your friends. In addition, you will become more dissatisfied with what you own, and feel critical about your 'average and plain' good looks. Since the beginning of time, gossip and storytelling have been a way for women to not only bond, but to convey what is socially acceptable and what isn't to build a communal, moral culture. Nonetheless, when we're unaware of how our minds work, we run the risk of our reactive emotions controlling us, and not our better judgment. Comparing and contrasting ourselves to others then becomes criticizing which alienates those who do not fit the tribe's expectations, thereby decreasing our level of unity.

When we watch shows and tabloids that zero in on the *worst* and *best* sides of a contestant, i.e. the sweet one, the pretty one, the manipulative one, etc., the categorization reinforces in our minds certain patterns of judgment and distrust. These shows warn our brains not to befriend women—for we may suffer betrayal, humiliation, or isolation. Moreover, our character becomes critical and soon enough we begin judging ourselves with those same squinted eyes. It's a vicious cycle of comparing and contrasting and in the process, we become more dissatisfied with ourselves. You may be mature enough to know the difference between Reality TV and reality, but consider how pervasive this drama of prejudice and competition is. It's a continuation of the fairytales we read as children: one man to compete for, one beautiful damsel in distress. It's not hard to see why sisters would turn against one another, tearing the jewels and gown off Cinderella to increase their chances of being chosen.

Whether we idolize or denigrate someone, what we're really doing is creating distance—whether it's done with the belief that he or she is either better than or worse than we are. We're not made perfect. If a camera followed us around every hour of the day, there would be some footage we wouldn't want to share. We're works in progress. Like every human being, we don't always say nor do the right thing. The times in which we act cruel, immature, or just plain stupid are truly opportunities for growth. Mistakes help us understand why it's important to have a good moral character. This is the *Paradox of Morality*. No one wants to appear judgmental, yet we judge everything in everybody.

The Third Parent

So why is beauty such an issue for women? Why, with all the

progress towards female empowerment is our beauty still a point of contention? We all grow up wanting to become what society idolizes and beauty is a big part of that. Advertising, television, radio, and magazines remind us every day what we should look like and how we fall short of that social expectation. When you pick up magazines, watch a television program, or look at a billboard where no one looks the way you do, you begin to wonder whether you fit in. Ultimately, you question whether you are enough as you are. It's hard not to feel the pressure when the world outside is telling you there are surgeries and treatments for girls and women *just like you* to look better.

By idolizing celebrities and models rather than peacemakers and powerful women, American capitalism appears to be more about fame attained by beauty and the adoration of men, than by hard work and perseverance. Moreover, as diverse as the American population is, we certainly don't embrace that diversity in advertising and entertainment. Those who are famous look very similar to one another. In fact, recently I came across a t-shirt that displayed a well-known black female singer, but I couldn't recognize her because her skin and blond hair looked completely Caucasian.

The media chants the same message each and every day through every dimension possible; that we just aren't good enough for true love until we look the best and have the best stuff. They have told us for years, the media simply delivers what we want to see, making media seem like a gauge of social attitudes. However, when only 3% of women have decision-making positions in media, we have to wonder: who is driving print, radio, and television programming? Encoded into our female DNA is risk aversion. Because fear is a protective mechanism, it's often reactive, using our more basic mental functions before moving up to more analytical areas of the brain. Fear and shame tactics therefore are the quickest, most effective way to grab our attention and affection, without much thought. Thus, when 97% of men are trying to boost up ratings and get products sold, it isn't hard to make the connection as to why exploiting women's increasingly threatened self-concept is such a lucrative business. A vicious cycle which Pat Mitchell, former president and CEO of PBS, best indicated as *the media* [being] both the message and the messenger. Media has imprinted in our minds since childhood that our dreams of happiness and love will be paid for—whether by ourselves or by a man—and the key to gaining access to that money is done with beautiful bodies, a bit of brains, and fame (no matter how high the price).

Looking in the Mirror

Psychological safety inside the relationships we foster is necessary in maintaining a healthy view of ourselves. Continuously watching programming and antagonistic tabloids trains our brains to view women as competitors. Witnessing twenty-five women compete for the affection of one (very lucky) *Bachelor,* ignites the neural mirroring emotional response of our ancestral brain. As we step into their shoes, we enter a mind portal where each character makes us evaluate what we would do in their situation. We all know, however, that how we *think* we would act in a given situation is much different from *actually living* through it. What may seem right or wrong from the outside can often be justified by the inside. Observing others prompts us to confront our own feelings by experiencing ***their*** emotions. We feel we understand because, in a sense, we've *been there* before. Connected in this way, despite the circumstance, as human beings we all experience jealously, sadness, and love.

In real life, this mirroring allows us to resonate with others. Watching others suffer or brighten up with elation turns on the same pain and pleasure centers of our brain. We identify our emotion in others and we recognize ourselves in them. Oftentimes, however, we fail to acknowledge that our own personal biases cloud our external observation. Each one of us has past traumas that affect present behavior. Let's not assume we know more than we do by summarizing our experiences into another's framework. A good rule of thumb to recognizing this limited view is checking to see whether we say definite statements, such as *she or he is **always** or **never*** (fill in the blank). There are many shades to an emotion and emotions frequently tie into our past. Keeping this in mind helps us all be more compassionate with one another. Typecasting a person to an emotional label such as jealous, judgmental, or naïve, transforms them into memes or mental constructs in our minds, obstructing us from seeing them as a complete person. Human beings were made to survive. The ability quickly to decipher with whom we can identify and who is a threat to our physical psychic safety is an instinct, but not one, which is always correct.

When we turn away from others, we close off our hearts and turn away from ourselves. Devaluing another person (on TV or otherwise) separates us. In an effort to gain psychological protection, we categorize *she is beautiful, but bitchy.* We reduce a complete person into a meme or metal construct in our mind to appease our own insecurities. The new title we create knocks her down the pedestal: *her flaw impedes her from being better than I am, so I'm still good enough to compete against her.* It's like an equalizer. We wrap ourselves in this emotional drama as we play out the roles of victim, friend, or foe... Although criticism and separation may calm anxiety temporarily, it can cause greater harm in the end. The same standard and measure we use on others becomes the same standard of measure we assume others will have of us.

Comparing and contrasting is predominately a feminine habit because it helps us bond with one another, defend the group, and discern our own values. The high estrogen in our physiology allows our empathetic nature to spill over into our relationships. It's our mama bear instinct to attack the aggressor and protect the cub. Learning to self-regulate the conflicting emotions within us strengthens our ability to understand that conflict in others.

Born Pretty

We're not all born pretty. My father, the archetype of the dark and handsome, Latin man didn't sleep for two days after my arrival. He was shocked his first-born child had been hit with the ugly stick. He couldn't understand how two attractive people could have made a not-so-pretty baby. Mind you, there wasn't anything abnormal about me, but whenever no one was looking, he would massage my nose in an effort to shape it into place. It took him twenty-one days (my hurt mother counted them), for him to show off his infant daughter. Needless to say, I'm thankful the nose is fine, there's absolutely nothing wrong with it (there never really was). Recently I caught my father staring at it.

When I noticed, he sheepishly laughed, but with pride emanating, saying, "You actually turned out to be a beautiful woman."

His first-born child had inherited his beautiful genes after all. I should probably take a moment here to say that beauty is of high value in our Latin culture—and when I had my own children, I was able to better understand that pride and apprehension. There's something in all of us that wants beautiful children, for numerous and varying reasons. Truth be told, as each of my children was born, a little bit of sadness crept up in noticing their minor imperfections. It wasn't that I didn't view them as beautiful or perfect, (quite the contrary), it was that I understood ridicule of these minor, infinitesimal imperfections might one day happen. I projected my own teasing of them without them having been alive an hour! In those first moments of gazing at every single one of their features, I vowed always to protect their little tender hearts and souls. Nevertheless, the truth is...I can't protect them from the entire world at all times.

The reality is, though, beauty is not only important in Latin culture. During each one of my pregnancies, people would approach Nick and me to say, "Oh my gosh, your children are going to be gorgeous." Many would actually look at us both and call out the features they wished our children would inherit from us: his eyelashes, my dark hair, etc... Then, as if it was a common courtesy, they turned to Nick to warn him of the tough road ahead if our baby bump turned out to be a girl. I would never wish ugly on my children, but I did hope neither child would be too pretty, too smart, too anything. Instead, I hoped each would be born with a kind heart, because it is from there humility and gratefulness is born. Nick, on the other hand, wanted really smart kids. Thankfully, our children came blessed with all those things. We are all born with just enough of what we're supposed to be. Having kids made me recognize this.

When it comes to looks, people scrutinize girls in particular. The competition is set up early on, and I saw it front and center almost immediately when Nazareen (my second) was born. People would say, "Nazareen is *soooo* beautiful." Then, without missing a beat, looking at Isadora standing next to her would add, "Oh, but you are even more beautiful than your sister," perhaps thinking that Isadora by instinct would feel competitive towards her sister. These same people loved my children and only said these things with good intentions, but what exactly were they trying to say?

I don't want my girls to be elitist about their good looks or believe they're more beautiful than others are. However, I also don't want them to feel less than average or inferior. It's unfortunate that beauty is a point of contention. We all have experienced that judgment. I remember the self-consciousness from having dark hair on my face. For a little girl to put a razor to her face is like admitting, "I am manly." I wanted to save my kids the ridicule of my youth. Being awkward and teased by people caused a lot of pain back then, but as an adult, it has given me so much more compassion. Watching people mock others brings me back to that time. Of course, I hope others do not tease my children, but what I really hope is that they understand that nobody is perfect.

Society's idea of beauty is all an illusion. Our imperfections are precisely what make us interesting. Ultimately, your body helps evolve your humanity. These bodies are instruments in which we experience prejudice and insecurities of the external that we try to overcome internally. Not appreciating our imperfections is not appreciating their value in our psychic development.

It's also important to acknowledge the pervasive misconception that pretty girls don't have it hard. Placed on a pedestal, pretty people are in a category of their own, as if they must have it easy and are not allowed to have insecurities or feel pain. In reality, judged for their externality rather than being valued for who they are internally, attractive, beautiful people can feel the hurt. The aging process can be difficult for beautiful women as they may find, perhaps for the first time, they no longer fit the illusory ideal. Sometimes looks can be so intimidating to people that the conventionally beautiful are sometimes treated as outcasts. It seems like a no-win situation, whether you're conventionally gorgeous, plain, or outright unattractive. How you look can have a positive or negative effect on your life—you choose which.

Every tease and every tear, uncovers for us the beauty of empathy. Rather than try to out-beauty women, laser hair removal was a way for me to look like everyone else. Being of Spanish decent has blessed me with Frida Kahlo looks: light skin and lots of dark, thick black hair. The older I became, the more looks (body hair) became an issue. Hair is what I first loved to hate about myself. Believing I was ugly and not allowing anyone to stand too close to my face, kept the sweet caresses of boy-friends away from my cheeks. The bleaching, tweezing, shaving, waxing, and Nair-ing were not part of my American girlfriends' grooming rou-tine. It felt like I was the only girl in the world with hair on her face.

My virtually hairless mother felt my hurt as adolescence brought on years of me looking down at my feet, rather than showing off my smile. By the time I graduated high school, she'd saved up much needed family money to afford laser hair removal treatments to assuage my insecurities. At the time, the treatments were very expensive and extremely painful; nonetheless, each agonizing red zap relieved the emotional pain I felt inside. To this day, I don't like facials. By instinct, self-consciousness returns and then as a learned habit, I remind myself I am much more than a hair on my chin.

This reflection of self-doubt and need for validation are already parts of my children's psyche: Nazareen is two and she demands her father's constant attention and approval. She asks over and over again, "Look at me, Baba," twirling in her tutu dress and smiling from ear to ear with lipstick all over her face. "Do I look beautiful like a princess, Baba!?" Then there's my five-year-old daughter Isadora. When she cut her gorgeous mane of hair, I was awestruck, as she proclaimed, "Isn't this exciting! I look like a fashionista, right?" A pang of pain punched me in the gut. Her jacked-up little boy haircut was far from being a "fashionista's bob." The haircut does have a name and the name is "Mullet." Instantly the bullying of childhood reverberated back. *Would they call her a boy?*

Looking at the dread painted across my face, large crocodile tears streamed down her own, as she realized her crown and glory (what she received constant praise for) was now splattered on our bamboo floor. Isadora recognized the hair would not grow back overnight and thought I was disappointed in her—in her beauty. In that one minute, she thought she'd lost her splendor. In my eyes, in my admiration, and in my words, I had defined beauty for my daughter. That pang hurt more! I held her, rocked her, affirming over and over again how lovely she truly is. Therefore, we mourned her locks of hair, but not her beauty. I would miss braiding her hair, making pigtails and a ballerina bun, but there are mothers who are buying wigs for their sick children. Ten minutes after the event, we headed to the salon.

Science and the Media

Some say we're the average of our friends. If the theory holds true and we apply that theory to our thought patterns (being the average of the shows, magazines, and Internet we watch), it explains a lot about why we think and act the way we do towards others. Remember the 1980s advertising campaign, "Don't hate me because I'm beautiful"? It was decades ahead of its time, or perhaps it was a profound foreshadowing to today's narcissism. What once was an insinuation of women's unspoken competitiveness is now a blatant display of criticism, degradation, and distrust. The nineties talk shows that focused on moral debates have now morphed into voyeuristic 'Real TV' dramas where women compete against one another to be the most talked about *Housewife* or chosen *Bachelorette*.

We live in a sophisticated age where brain science, entertainment, and advertising intertwine more and more. As a result, neuro-marketing has given those with monetary interests, greater insights, and tools into manipulating our emotional hot buttons. Subliminal messaging is nothing new, but as Reality TV brings the viewer into the screen, and the fate of reality stares into the hands of viewers, it's become harder and harder to discern when, where, and what we are being sold. Consumerism—the materialistic insatiable desire for more, feeds off of glorified egos, exposing anxieties, and subjecting us to what we fear most. It does this by breaking down our sense of belonging and togetherness, making us feel as though we are not good enough to be accepted as we are.

The goal of media is not to draw us closer. Our argumentative culture is divisive. It dichotomizes and polarizes people into opposing camps. The reason these shows are so popular is that they entice our senses through our love for drama. Those with whom we come in contact mold our personalities. Feeling our emotions enliven us whether they are a product of a real or imagined relationship. These shows are dramatizations and not real life. There's little room to appreciate the differences of others when we view them as adversaries. It's like looking at a cutout display of a person; you only see one side, but if we bothered to look behind her, we would dismantle the illusion.

To our mechanical brain, becoming attached to characters on T.V. is not different from living out the storylines and dramas of our friends. Embedded deep within our ancestral coding are instincts, many times sexual and psychological, which have helped form our unconscious habits. Judgment is natural, but unobserved judgment is dangerous. Being unaware of these primal reflexes has given marketers greater control of our psyches than we have of ourselves. This is not conspiracy theory—it's a fact. By not educating ourselves on how to better control our minds, we've allowed media to pump our brains with high doses of Consumerism steroids, socialized to crave bigger, better, and faster doses of excitement and pleasure.

Consumerism is just a steppingstone towards the bigger addiction—sensationalism. By glamorizing the immoral we have become desensitized to what was once controversial. For instance, when we become sexually aroused or watch acts of violence our automatic nervous system goes into overdrive igniting something primal in us. We get stuck in a loop of wanting immediate relief or pleasure—each time we scratch that itch the need for higher doses of that guilty pleasure grows like poison ivy, and we look for more shock and awe programming to give us that rush once more.

An Evolutionary Function

Like the tend and befriend trigger caused by babies and puppies, there is a legitimate evolutionary purpose and function for beauty. Beauty is the way in which natural selection ensured genes would live onto the next generation. Attracting the provision and protection of the strongest and most virile men meant securing the physical safety of a woman, which in turn safeguarded the children and the elders for whom women cares. Therefore, while men compete with fists and financial status, women have competed with beauty and words. Women, often thought of as having a risk-averse brain, while conversely, men's brains are more step-thinking and linear.

Fertility and sex are primal qualities. Men do fifty push-ups before a date to pump up their muscles while women wear Spanx, a push-up bra, and lipstick. It's a dance. Media is aware of our impulsive weaknesses and so capitalizes on sexualized content. As an example, it's of no coincidence that women who have a certain hip-to-waist ratio become cast as models and spokeswomen. Youthful proportions are eye-catching, not simply because socially we define beauty in a certain size, but because at a very basic, neurological level our brain encodes an hourglass figure as fertile in the mind's computer. Women, too, can fall prey to body before brains. Likewise, men's masculine features (muscle strength and voice) have been noted to be more appealing at the point of ovulation presumably to motivate women to attract the stronger gene pool. To support the notion that neuro-biology and our species evolution is always controlling us, when women pass their ovulation period, men who have more subtle features become more appealing to change our focus from seeking a manly man to a monogamy man.

Likewise, the female brain is constantly projecting future risks so reviewing other women is a primal instinct. Comparing and contrasting our attractiveness to that of other women is a defensive move to guard against obstacles in our romantic conquests. Nonetheless, as primal as it may be for us to survey the intentions and character of other women, it goes against our nature to alienate or disparage another human being. We no longer live at a time of scarce resources where we must fight for a man to feed our young. Women weren't just sitting around in a harem waiting for the one man in the tribe to come and make them feel special. Besides, even in hunter-gatherer days, men had to work for *It*.

'Fun'draising

Laser hair removal changed my life. The experience was so profound in helping me feel less self-conscious that I decided to open a laser aesthetics clinic of my own. This, I thought, would be the best way I could use the insecurities, which had plagued me for the good, and help others see themselves more fully. The procedures did in fact help hundreds of women and men feel more attractive and experience a similar metamorphosis. Navigating the world of beauty however, was both more thought provoking and morally challenging than I had imagined.

For instance, a considerable amount of highschool girls entered the clinic wanting to preserve their prepubescent look by permanently removing hair in regions that signified their physical maturation, but their brains had yet to fully mature. I sometimes wonder if any of them regret not having an option to change it up *down there* now that the au naturelle look is making a comeback. Do they think of their cha-cha's as looking passé now that American Apparel puts an un-groomed mannequin on display and Cameron Diaz reminds us that pubic hair is the norm, not a trend? It wasn't just women, men of all ages, too, pay for permanent hair removal in their nether parts. Patients openly spoke of wanting to fashion themselves after the adult stars their partners admired.

Perhaps the most morally taxing experience was when a potential patient asked that we consider a new type of payment plan. We already had interest-free financing and in case she didn't qualify, we explained we'd gladly work out a payment plan. She had a better idea... Apparently, her recent breast augmentation had been entirely paid for by an Internet site that describes itself as the following: *a social networking website that provides a fun, safe, and debt-free alternative to expensive breast augmentation* loans. The site is comprised of three groups of people: ladies, contributors, and surgeons. *Contributors* and *Ladies* enter a web exchange agreement where donors and recipients are not required to **do or display** anything with which they're uncomfortable... Take into consideration however, the escrow account set up and publicly displaying both the monetary amount needed to collect, and a time count next to the ladies' profile pictures and videos. Competition is fierce as hundreds of other ladies try to get their boobs funded. Suffice it to say they're not dressed up in burkas and relying on their personalities alone to get the job done. Here is America's obsession with breasts in full glory. Our patient proudly reported she had reached her goal faster than any other lady in the site at the time. How about that for our competitive archaic brain?

Unfortunately, for her, our clinic did not have such a program. Reflecting back on conversations we had with patients, the undertones of the admonitions (from bleaching to vaginoplasty) made this laser-aesthetic clinic sometimes feel more like a sex therapist's office. In a study of more than 2,000 women conducted by Dr. Laura Berman and Dr. Mieke Ana Windecker found that women who had the most positive view of their vaginas testified to having the most sexual energy and were better able to achieve an orgasm. Sadly, behind our clinic's closed doors, it became more and more obvious that a growing number of women (mostly young women) are ashamed of vaginas that don't replicate those displayed in adult entertainment.

A new *designer vagina* trend has emerged, scrutinizing women's most private parts. Vaginal rejuvenation, the combination of labiaplasty and vaginoplasty meant to tighten genital muscles and diminish the appearance of the vulva, has become one of plastics more sought out surgeries. According to a 2011 review published by the *International Society of Sexual Medicine,* 87 percent of vaginal rejuvenation patients opt for the surgery for purely aesthetic reasons. In 2007, *The American College of Obstetricians and Gynecologists* issued the following warning: "Women should be informed about the lack of data supporting the efficacy of these procedures [vaginoplasties and labiaplasties] and their potential complications including infection, altered sensation, dyspareunia, adhesions, and scarring." Two years later, note the following statistic: According to an estimate from the *American Academy of Cosmetic Surgeries,* there was a 50 percent increase from 2008 to 2009 of these types of surgeries and more than 60 percent of the women were between 20 and 39-years-old.

Vaginal rejuvenation has helped many women gain self-confidence. Many patients receive these types of surgeries as a result of episiotomies and extensive weight loss. However, there are women who opt for the procedure purely for the satisfaction of their partners without contemplating what it will do to their own libido and health.

Women are not prepackaged in an assembly line; we all look different. To celebrate that difference one artist displayed 30 different vaginas so women could see themselves in the diagram and nullify their concern of their bodies being ugly, abnormal, or inadequate. Bringing awareness to pornography's effects on women's psyche is an important issue to explore. Suffice it to say, our sexuality is an important component of our identities and accepting who we are, as we are, is central to our sensuality and sexuality. In the documentary, **"*The Perfect Vagina*"**, the camera followed a women's support group in the UK who, in order to come to terms with their labial dysmorphia, had an artist cast their vaginas in plaster and then make molds so they could objectively observe them separate from their bodies. Considering their sculptures amongst the rest, they were able to appreciate their positive features rather than the imperfections that had embarrassed them.

CHAPTER 3

Hippity-Hop

"There's a place in France where the naked ladies dance, and a hole in the wall where boys [men] can watch it all..."
- song written by Sol Bloom (who later became a US Congressman)

*I*f France has mastered the art of gourmet food and seduction, the United States has mastered the art of fast food and fast-sex. With time, the Free Love movement of art, music, and literature replaced love for sex, and gave way to the sexual revolution of the 70s with its flashy disco balls and unabated promiscuity. Now, fast-forward to the hook-up culture of this Millennium, where the pornification of America has candy-wrapped sexuality into a new brand of chauvinism (or better said show-vinism)—with artificial climaxes and addictively numbing foreplay.

Madonna to Miley

We're not just peeking into some sort of erotic dance. Glamorized for all to blatantly see, the raunch culture received its official inauguration at the 2013 VMAs when Miley Cyrus's spectacle with Robin Thicke set the new standard to beat-out (or twerk-out). *"Me and Robin the whole time said, 'You know we're about to make history right now.'"*

Miley went on to say, *"You're thinking about it more than I thought about it when I did it. Like, I didn't even think about it 'cause that's just*

me. I don't pay attention to the negative because I've seen this play out so many times. How many times have we seen this play out in pop music? Madonna's done it. Britney's done it. Every VMA's performance, that's what you're looking for; you're wanting to make history." Herein is the problem: straining to make history by any means possible without the responsibility of thought.

By comparison, it's hard to believe Madonna singing 'Like a Virgin' on stage was controversial in its day. Maybe Miley's right, maybe we're all just too uptight. Music is part of pop-culture, it's a social gauge of what we're willing to sanction as appropriate. Drugs, Sex, Rock & Roll are a result of humanity's desire for transcendence. We all yearn to feel uninhibited, spiritually connected, and free. Nonetheless, however free we may want to be, consequences follow choices. We're accountable for our moral obligation to society. MTV has taken that responsibility to heart as their *16 and Pregnant* reality show has made teens press their eye against the hole in the wall to take a critical look at the other side of having irresponsible sex. In fact, a new study accredited the show with scaring young, would-be mothers straight, and decreasing teen pregnancy in our country.

For as long as we're alive, there will be very real humanitarian issues linked to sexuality. As early as 1917, the first birth control activist, Margaret Sanger, was arrested for running a Planned-Parenthood Clinic in Brooklyn. Today, with more than 70 anti-abortion provisions enacted last year, widely varying public opinion, and the controversial Obamacare birth-control debate still pending, we have left sex education in the hands not of education, but media.

"Strike a Pose...Vogue, Vogue, Vogue"

When feedback from negative press receives the applause, it's easy to be caught in a cycle of mindlessness. Miley is well on her way to rivaling Madonna's three-decade career of ever changing identities as she becomes one of America's most followed musicians in social networks. While promoting her personal documentary, *Miley: The*

Movement, the young singer reminds us of the magnitude our *first idols* carries and how their music played in the background of our youth."*... even if you don't know it seeps into your brain, into your soul, into your spirit. That makes you who you are, your DNA.*" Miley could not be more accurate.

A lot has transpired since Miley's first idol, Britney Spears kissed Madonna and Christina Aguilera on stage. Menage-a-trios innuendos have escalated to overt sexual displays, producing utter shock and awe. As a response to her child star fame turning to infamy, Miley asserts, *"People change; you don't know who you are going to be."* Miley has her eye on the prize, echoing young Madonna's aspirations to *conquer the world*. If Madonna can change from material girl, to mogul, to mom, why can't Miley? In our culture, holding sarcasm and critiques in higher esteem than praise and encouragement is the norm. Snarky comments make us appear intelligent, funny, and witty. However, each sarcastic, derogatory remark muddies our reputation. Soon we're expected to continue the charade—lest we be seen as hypocrites or fakes. As people evolve, there are new lessons learned and with that learning, there's more responsibility. Positive change is not only possible, but also expected. It takes far more effort to be positive and conscientious. To paraphrase spiritual teacher Eckhart Tolle, "Negativity is not intelligent, it fails to see the connection of all things. Sarcasm, cynicism, and mockery may be evocative but its negative effects are far-reaching."

Of course, our identities do not hold at a constant. Our ideas about sex in our twenties aren't what they are in our thirties. In adolescence, we think sexy means skimpy and tight, with boobs hiked up to our chins—but soon enough we come to find that sensuality is much more interesting than the obvious in-your-face sexual advertising. Our hook-up culture has convinced us that what men want are pseudo bi-sexual girlfriends—women who like to play with women, but who only want to be loyal to men. We need to stop making a mockery out of sex and love. Dramatizing ourselves as straight lesbians contends with our personal integrity while simultaneously disrespecting those who authentically live out their sexual preferences and who still struggle for acceptance.

In 1948, Alfred Kinsey introduced the idea that our sexual inclinations lie within a spectrum. Before religion began moralizing sex, evolutionary psychologists surmised that the need for many women to support themselves and their children might have led to more sexual flexibility. In nomadic days, when male partners were killed, or in search of food for long periods of time, it was of real value to women to integrate into a poly-amorous or same sex coupling to raise their young. Some estimate two-thirds of heterosexual women hold an attraction towards other women and to further authenticate the hypothesis, many lesbians report having some level of attraction for men.

It wasn't until the 80s and 90s that art, fashion, and music socialized a more open-minded view of sexuality. Artists like Madonna used their celebrity to pry open the taboos of sexual identity and self-love and made them vogue. Let's not burn Miley at the stake. She is, after all, right about one thing: the new millennium has brought about a movement. We are the largest generation of women to date and we are affecting change. So let's make that movement mindful and conscientious.

Sexuality is as complex as individuality; incapable of being classified and checked off in a small, self-contained, unyielding, homo/hetero box. Moreover, both men and women's sexuality is evolving all over the world. Not only is humanity as a whole more tolerant, we're sincerely more empathetic and compassionate friends. Being straight, bisexual, gay, or transgendered, is a *dimension* of a personality, not the *definition* of a person. While there are many transsexual and transgendered individuals who still struggle with the stigma of their sexual identities, society is now reaching out for deeper understanding. There are family support groups, hormone therapies, and sex-surgeries now available for those who feel trapped inside bodies that don't fully represent who they are inside.

There's so much more left to do than just consuming fast, free sex. If you want to be a part of true social progress with real political and humanitarian clout, then continue the sexual liberation movement onwards. Same-sex marriage is the civil rights issue of our times. When, as a nation, we can acknowledge we all have the right to love who we love, and be who we are, it is then that a Movement of Unconditional Love will reunite us.

Accepting Our Vulnerability

Being comfortable in our skin, in touch with nature and its surroundings, and enjoying moments of pleasure truly is the essence of feminine sensuality. Our bodies are beautiful instruments, designed to walk us through the cycle of life. They're not solely ours, because they're also the vessel we use to share love with others; out of our bodies we make love, procreate, and feed our young. For this reason, men and women are wired differently. We have a more contextual way of pleasing Eros; intimacy stems from the vulnerable parts of us feeling accepted and safe. For women to feel truly sexually nourished, our bodies request a sense of physical abandonment where the moment of exaltation transcends us away from feeling self-conscious—to such degree that our brain shuts down (so to speak) while we orgasm. Anthropologists link this phenomena to the hunter and gatherer days when women sought men they could trust, lest they become pregnant and therefore less capable of caring for themselves alone.

However, when we take into account how often we have denied our feminine identity and readjusted our romantic natures by adopting a more masculine approach to sexuality, the implications of our ignorance of how our bodies work can have strong implications in our sexual pleasure, identity, and overall self-concept. Date-night courtships are meaningful to coupling. As we feast off our meals, our bodies experience physiological changes that imitate sexual arousal; our pulse rate rises, our skin becomes more susceptible, some of us even sweat. Well, pornography is like drive-through sex. Like a fast food joint, it can (briefly) appease a craving, but a four-course candle lit dinner is much more gratifying. We don't always have the time for candlelight, but there is a place in-between a five-minute-quickie and a 24-hour *sex-capade*. Again, I am not saying we should be puritans, or only have missionary sex with people with whom we want to live happily ever after. After all, sex without the fear of having a lifetime of attachment to a baby or the father is the pill's greatest asset. Sex should be playful and pleasurable for its own sake.

According to Naomi Wolfe:

"Dopamine is the ultimate feminist chemical in the female brain. When a woman's dopamine system is optimally activated (as it is in the anticipation of great sex), a woman's knowing of what turns her on (sexually and otherwise) strengthens her sense of focus and motivation levels, energizes her in setting goals. All those effects are involved in dopamine activation. It is accurate to say that if you activate your dopamine system in seeking out great sex as a woman, your brain can take those heightened capabilities of energy and focus it into other areas of your life."

Teen males run readily and steadily towards their sexual peak up until their early twenties. They then pass that baton to women, who reach their sexual pinnacle in their early thirties. While men's libido declines over time, women's remains constant. There certainly are those who are more sexual than others are (**women who have high-levels of Dopamine and Testosterone for example typically are more sexual than the average),** but sexual or not, we must connect to something more than just a perfunctory make-believe idea of pleasure to be able to fully express our feminine sensuality.

Despite American women having more sex than ever before, our sexual arousal has actually gone down. Put candidly, we're having more sex and fewer orgasms. We think we've outsmarted men by beating them at their own game, but each of our authentic natures eventually emerges and the game of friends with benefits runs dry. Exploring our sexual identity by un-attaching our feelings to partners we like but do not trust, has made our long-term *engagements* dissatisfying. If we pretend to reach climax or feign enjoyment simply to aggrandize a partner's ego, we're not really there; we're not a true partner in the act of sex. Sex is about connecting, be it with a partner or self.

With the Internet at the curious fingertips of boys that soon enough become men—girls and women have a new competitor in the dating arena. Sonya Thompson from the University of Alberta shares a disheartening Study [showing] 1 in 3 Boys [are] Heavy Porn Users. (Study, 5 March 2007). The powerful hormone chemicals released during orgasm imprint within our molecular memory patterns of thought and reward. In an age of sexting, Internet dating, and 'fun'draising sexual exchanges, men's minds are becoming hardwired for over-stimulation. Becoming desensitized to traditional sex is becoming a real problem for both sexes. Women now find themselves trying to gain sexual rank over the make-believe. This is an important point to take into consideration as the understanding of sexual propriety is being taught over the Internet, with personas that are far from authentic.

When we try to re-enact what we see on adult films, it strips us of true emotional intimacy, and makes the act of taking off our clothes more perilous. Pornography in all its forms is a performance, not a how-to manual and certainly not an act of true love-making. Be it on print or film, the tone and texture of these reenactments or characters targeted towards men are distinctly different from those targeted to female consumers. The male visual cortex is highly entangled in sexual overtures, thus they are much more likely to conjure up specific body parts and images that arouse, making fetishes more appealing to the masculine mind then to the feminine mind. In extreme cases, the continued release of neurochemicals in the pleasure and reward centers of our brains, resulting from over-indulgence, can trigger an addiction, but unlike drugs or alcohol where the affinity is towards more and more, those who have sexual addictions crave more and more novelty. That need for variety can land young impressionable boys, who've never been on a real date with a real girl onto sites that display a very different picture between what foreplay, sex, and love actually are.

Thankfully, there are therapies to help reverse hypersexual conditions. Nevertheless, sexual addiction is highly stigmatized and until people accept it as a real disorder, sex-addicted men and women will be hard-pressed to seek out help and admit to their partners that they have a problem.

Completely Exposed

Nakedness is our most vulnerable state. We hold our breath hoping our bodies alone—in all our perfect imperfections—are enough to bring the transcendental moment of ecstasy to our partners. Accepted when we are most vulnerable, we're likely to apply that learned confidence in our interactions outside of our private quarters.

Expectations lead to disappointment some say; I generally disagree with this statement, but my *first time* was like going to a gemologist with a very special stone and he not recognizing its tremendous value. This first experience with the pleasure of sex was shared with a giant 24" x 36" voluptuous bikini image of Jenny McCarthy on the wall next to my boyfriend's bed. (In case you missed the book cover... there's not one part of me that resembles Jenny McCarthy.) Frustrated that his real-life naked girlfriend wasn't enough to get him aroused, he closed his eyes, took his hands off me, placed them on the wall, opened his eyes, and admiringly stroked Jenny's flat, hard, make-believe legs. Yes, the poster, and when Jenny didn't do the trick, he stood up, went to his closet, and took out a magazine.

Seeing the tears flowing down my cheeks he said, "What? Don't feel bad, these are models!"

My response was, "I'm sorry, I'll start working out."

At some point, however, in those first soirées, his own gemstones began to decrease in value. I will never know his memory of the experience, but I truly hope, at some point, he was able to stand in salutation for a living, breathing, real-life woman, and not just the cover of a magazine.

Women hold on to sexual encounters like Polaroid pictures, placing them up like cards, one behind the other. When we have a long enough list of experiences that normalize events such as these, which make us feel as though we aren't enough, we tap them like domino pieces on a line. We're left flattened and afraid.

Our Bodies, Ourselves... the Next Stage

When our bodies change, we change. At each stage, from girlhood, to adolescence, young adult, to motherhood; these phases of women-hood bring with it curiosity, challenge, and exploration. A myriad sexually explicit dances animate the cultures of the world. It's simply carnal. *Twerking* is not new, even bonobo monkeys understand the power of a good booty shake. That type of cultural variety can be appreciated in South Florida, my home turf. It is a multicultural, multiethnic, melting pot entangling you with its urban hip-hop culture, as we all come together on the dance floor provocatively shaking our rumps with strong stimulating sounds, designed to provoke sexual tension.

The music is intoxicating, the vibration seductive, and the lyrics in large part ignored. With beats that "Make your booty go (**smack**)...," men objectify women and women in return objectify men. We antagonize them in an erotic dance of, *come hither...* and then feel powerful when we say, 'No, just kidding. You don't deserve *this.*' By *this*, I mean, sex. Who do you think does the ***smacking***? When we use sex as a tool to aggrandize our egos, we all lose. Degrading lyrics fan our embers of distrust towards one another. To a more sober mind, this sexually explicit music doesn't always sound so good. It's like having the words you said in a moment of drunken passion, in the wee hours of the night, broadcasted on the microphone at Sunday morning mass.

Becoming a mother sobered me up, real quick. The quarters inside the deep crevasses of the car seats seem to shrink as orgasmic sounds are remixed into music beats and the sweet voices of my little girls shout lines I have once sung. If you've not yet experienced it, let me just say, it's horrifying and embarrassing to hear a three- and five-year-old harmonize together at the top of their lungs, ***"Do what you want with my body!!!... Do what you want... Do what you want."***

Should I have the 'talk' before or after the song is over?

It's just a song.

No, I need to turn the station off.

—And make it more obvious? Make it a bigger deal when they beg to switch it back?

Being a parent is mentally exhausting. Things that used to seem trivial now seem like matters of safety. The time will come when it will be necessary to fully explain sexual propriety—how, long ago, I made a vow to shake *"What **My** Mama Gave **Me"*** for their father—a man that respected me just as much as he respects my moves. Dancing is fun, and hip-hop/urban sounds are great. It's also great to filter out songs and tradeoffs that are truly debasing. Nothing is louder than the silence of the ching-ching no longer endorsing derogatory songs, or contractual drinks at the bar. We don't have to stop dancing, stand in a corner with our arms crossed, and pout. We also don't have to put-out because someone bought us a drink for our booty shaking time.

The Beastie Boys, despite their misogynistic frat boy mentality, were the background music of my youth. B-Boys' music wasn't just objectifying to women, they perpetuated the idea that masculinity not only repelled homosexuality, but had disdain for it (unless it was hot lesbians, of course). A fan base of immature, impressionable kids that thought it was all just funny and cool, changed what began first as a parody into their band's brand, eventually making them both rich and popular. Fortunately, the Beastie Boys matured and have since apologized publicly for their misconduct, facing fans, and saying, "Time healed our stupidity." They changed offensive lyrics and encouraged other music artists to follow suit. Once, at a music festival the Beastie Boys even asked a collaborating band to scratch a song out of their set because it was particularly offensive. When the band refused, the Beasties retaliated by saying they would make their own fans aware of their difference in opinion. This progressive attitude was not well received. Some said the B-Boys were more concerned with women rights than freedom of speech. However, isn't standing up for humanity a principle worth defending?

Think about this for a minute… judging others by notoriety alone distances us from uncovering something much richer. Who people are publicly oftentimes conflicts with who they are privately. The stories people gravitate to the most are not necessarily the mistakes, or the accolades, but those, which demonstrate personal integrity, which inspires us to grow.

All we're ever able to do is give the best of ourselves to the world and let it be deciphered as it may. If ever you feel stuck in an identity that gives external gains but no true intrinsic value, sometimes it is of most value to find a space away from admirers. Then avow: *"I'll be here when you are ready to evolve with me, but in the meantime, I am not allowing you, popularity, or my past, to define who I am now or who I am on my way to 'being.' Even if that means, you will no longer be part of my life."* It couldn't have been easy to have long-standing fans walk away, when the Beastie Boys' lyrics changed, affirming their now more humanitarian efforts. *"I want to say something that is long overdue/The disrespect to women has got to be through/To all the mothers and sisters and wives and friends/I want to offer my love and respect to the end."* Nevertheless, a new set of followers joined the fans that had made the B-Boys mature. They emblemize self-respect and integrity, reminding us how our growth choices authenticate a more humane, reincarnated self.

Namaste, Little Bunny

Namaste in Hinduism is translated to mean, 'I bow to the divine in you'. A common practice inside yoga classes is to greet those we meet with this sacred gesture. It's a beautiful exchange that reminds us to let go of our prejudices and remember the soul, which lives in us all—a spirit that is immeasurable and saintly. Sitting down with legs crossed, placing my hands in prayer pose, I bent my forehead to the floor when a sweet-faced, 10-year-old girl caught my attention. She was what most young girls are at age ten—she had a boyish figure and an excited spirit. You could tell she was happy to be in a grown-up yoga class with her mom. Spreading out her mat, she caught my eye through the mirror's reflection.

I smiled at her, but this bow to the ground was not a true Namaste greeting. The action provided me an opportunity to gather my thoughts. As my head lay on the dewy floor, I tried to sooth my anger and sadness towards her. In the moment, I'd smiled at the little girl, I'd also become reflexively infuriated by her yoga-wear. In a place where the intention is to appreciate your body and accept who you are, she wore a spaghetti strapped tank top with a giant neon pink, iconic *Playboy* emblem. She might as well have been naked to me. Was this what she thought being older meant? Was her selection an attempt to fit in?

This was perhaps the best yogic experience I've had to date since I spent the rest of the class time exercising the calming down of emotions, trying to let go of the urge to put an oversized sweatshirt on top her neon pink bunny. How far has society come that ten-year-old girls are now walking advertisements for nudity? It's certainly fair, at least to say, pornography has become mainstream. Brown University's Health promotion site reports children as young as five-years-old have an understanding of what is and is not culturally desirable and shaming, even assigning negative connotations to figures of larger children. What will happen to that little girl's smile when she realizes her square and fleshy body probably will not naturally grow into that biologically unattainable Playboy standard?

Maybe women who are depicted in media and glorified as *sexy and hot* are different shades and different heights, but by and large media conveys a cultural standard—not easily attained without the aid of dieting, plastic surgery, and good genes. In 2011, Abercrombie and Fitch marketed the *push-up triangle bikini top* to girls as young as seven-years-old. Self-objectification is common among young girls. Studies show that if that little girl in yoga class is like the average American tween, in three more years she will be unhappy with her body. However, if she's somewhat able to escape that self-consciousness by age seventeen, the chances of self-depreciation jump to 78%.

Playboy's brand is about celebrating the beauty of women, not prepubescent girls. Undeniably, Playboy has broken down stereotypes to celebrate the beauty and sexuality of athletes, black women, and pregnant women. However, as pornography goes mainstream, and *Girls Gone Wild* becomes a rite of passage, little girls grow up having a misconception of what sexuality and sensuality really is; the appreciation of femininity and transcending out of our bodies and beyond our senses.

Pick Your Fantasy

True empowerment is much more than exhibitionism and sex appeal. I'm not a prude, or here to regulate moralistic sex. In fact, I have a dancing pole in my own bedroom to work out. (Okay, obviously I don't use it to work out!) It's a character's prop, so to speak, as it *can* feel liberating in fact to take on a character and have it bring out a secret part of our personality that would ordinarily be too shy to come out. The real deal here is eroticism has its place, as does fantasy and play. It's fun! Putting on a persona for a night is one thing, consistently denying your own pleasure or authentic nature for the sake of admiration is quite another. As pornography becomes pervasive in everyday interplay, i.e. pole dancing workouts, Playboy reality shows, and adult film stars gaining rank over mainstream celebrities, a new pressure for real women to compete with porn stars has emerged.

The prepubescent woman—a half woman/half girl figure which is voluptuous on the top and tiny, tiny on the bottom—has become increasingly popular as adult films allow us to visually survey the idealized woman. Nevertheless, let's all acknowledge that although there may be an *ideal* for pornography, it's not the same as men's ideal. Men, who truly love women and the female form, don't want a caricature of a woman—they want to feel flesh and know it's real. Men don't hold a caste system of attraction. They see a woman, are attracted to her, see another, and are attracted to her too. This *who is (prettier, sexier, hotter)* game lives within the female mind. Women who are shock-full of artificial components heighten senses only for a moment. That rise to the visual cortex sells like candy, but pornography is not an exposé of the masculine mind.

Pornography arouses lust; it's the nearing into what we don't actually have and don't fully know. Lust is distance, love and intimacy is closeness. To be sure, it can be empowering to take care of our natural urges on our own. Masturbation detaches emotion so an independent sexual experience can be possible, although, as with all good things, moderation is the key. Women, too, can suffer from an over-indulgence of additive stimulants (such as vibrators or performance enhancing drugs). This can be a treacherous competitor for men.

Leaked sex tapes and photographs have taken the virtually unknowns to everyday household stardom by exploiting sex as the fastest track to empowerment. Celebrity adult film star, Jenna Jameson, reveals a different truth in her memoir. Behind the curtain of the adult industry lie many personal inner battles and compromises.

Empowered women are sexy, no doubt—and that can't be bought or feigned. Displaying your ta-tas on the pages of a magazine may make a statement, one that under the right light and context can be empowering. So can wearing a Burka. Many Muslim women feel proud and empowered by not having the distraction of their bodies with which to contend. After the photo shoots and film are gone, we look into the mirror, into ourselves. Sexual empowerment is liberating only as a form of individualized self-expression.

CHAPTER 4

It's Just Business

"The greatest untapped resource of our land—the land of the free—is the collective mind of the American woman: the embodiment of compassion and unity. To mine the wealth of her voice and her vote is to give rise to a new, more empowered nation, hence truly becoming indivisible, bearing liberty, and justice for all women and all men."

Solange Jazayeri

*P*lease unfold, Lady Justice! Consider for a moment that she is blindfolded to prevent herself from witnessing the devaluation of women and girls. Women's innate nature is to bring people together to grow in relationships and to support and encourage one another. Yet, our unified voice is not being heard – the scales of justice are still off balance. Our sensationalist culture would have us believe the women's liberation movement has made us successful enough to *have it all,* if only we want it and work hard for it. But, can we? Can we truly have it all if our financial opportunities are what determine whether we will pay attention to the tick tock of our biological clock?

Fearing that motherhood will slide us back a few notches in the corporate ladder, twenty-somethings are delaying motherhood today only to slow down (or quit) tomorrow. By our thirties, we find ourselves at crossroads standing between our careers, our need to build a home, and our personal fulfillment. Balance is the Holy Grail, but without a road map, we lose ourselves in our chasing of an unrealistic dream.

Promotions are important, but so is saving enough time to evaluate romantic interests, not as distractions but potential lifelong partners.

Said bluntly, career driven women are finding their *It's Just Lunch Dates* to be more like paternity interviewing. According to the Centers for Disease Control and Prevention's National Vital Statistics Report, the number of mothers between the ages of 35 and 39 has increased 150 percent since the 1970s.

Chasing fulfilling and financially prosperous careers has us taking our fertility for granted , expecting everything else to eventually find its appropriate slot in our schedule. As we grow inside our professional identities, we also grow older. Not since the advent of birth control has family and career planning come under such scrutiny as we evaluate the investment in egg freezing and in vitro-fertilization versus our professional advancement. Our biological clock is the stopwatch to our race. The growing trend in fertility insurance points to the monetary gains of our early careers, having to pay for our baby making later in life.

It was in 2007 when my alarm clock finally went off. Nick and I wanted to create a life together. Parenthood we thought was the final frontier of adulthood. Kids would be the key to that unconditional happiness money had not yet fulfilled. After years of trying to *protect myself*, it was shocking that making a baby was much more arduous than anticipated. I went from not wanting any children to stand in my way, to being panic-stricken that I'd taken fertility for granted. In typical form, I now wanted what I couldn't have. My fear response ignited. It was hard to imagine I could not have what had been promised to me. Therefore, a strong fight with my ovaries, body, and mind began. I do not mean that in a metaphorical sense. Fertility treatments changed my character and internal dialogue overnight. Exchanging birth control for hormone therapy catapulted me into an existential crisis.

Clomid, a drug the size of a grain of rice, changed my neuro-chemistry in inexplicable ways. At first, everything was very confusing. What I knew to be true became upside down with each dosage. My personality felt foreign; my perceptions and moods were contingent on the side effects of this new little pill. Stuck between fear and neurotic thinking, I felt disconnected from myself, and those around me. No longer a workaholic, I mindlessly flipped channels in bed, watching reality stars live out their lives to avoid living out my own. I was a different person all together, irritable, and bitchy, with only one thing on the mind: *the business of making a baby*... baby... got to get the baby. Now it seemed obvious that my happiness and who I was became contingent upon my hormones and chemistry, not financial success. Truth be told, despite all I had achieved, I knew deep inside me I had never felt satisfied or at peace by work alone. So, then what defined me? This tiny pill had changed everything.

My body had once given me all the signs that it was time to have a child, but I had ignored it and instead I got a puppy. The cave woman inside made the need to have a child visceral. Sex was transactional. Nick was a piece of meat, a means to an end, more than a want. At a time when we expected to be the closest, we felt distant and apart. In one particular fight Nick yelled, "I don't want to inseminate you right now either! But we have to do it!" The comment was well deserved, trust me. Thank G-d this wasn't the night of our firstborn's conception. My heart really goes out to couples who split up at this time. Going through infertility brings all personal issues and emotions to the surface. It felt as if I were being punished for having been so career focused all this time. Now my achievements paled in comparison to this massive failure—not being woman enough to have a baby.

This experience served as a catalyst for my questioning where female empowerment truly lay and more pertinent to my identity crisis—who am I, if not career-driven? Am I still ambitious, independent, and successful? My modern brain was competing against my ancestral brain and I stood in between both. Communication and leadership had been the focus of my graduate studies...and now I found myself asking who (or what force) was truly communicating and leading me; was it society, hormones/brain, primal biology?!

You may not have an identity crisis as a result of infertility or motherhood, but if what you value most is autonomy over connection, financial success over experiences, inevitably one day you will find yourself lost. When you do, please remember the words of Erika Harris, "It is good to feel lost... because it proves you have a navigational sense of where *Home is*. You know that a place that feels like *being found* exists. And maybe your current location isn't that place but, Hallelujah, that unsettled, uneasy feeling of lost-ness just brought you closer to it."

Front and Center

Although women have proven to be strong contenders in today's economy, our successes have come at the expense of downplaying our biological and psychological needs. As a result, we have a lower sense of well-being. A study conducted by Wharton School of Business at the University of Pennsylvania entitled, *The Paradox of Declining Female Happiness,* it was determined that despite more work opportunities than ever before, and forty years of feminism under our belt, self-actualization still seems outside our grasp. The research reports a consistent decline in women's subjective happiness since the 1970s. The two professors responsible for this study, known as the go-to couple on matters of divorce, childrearing, and family economics, Betsey Stevenson and Justin Wolfers, suggest that a reason for this unhappiness could be the added responsibilities women have assumed in the workplace and in the home. As opportunities increased, so did expectations. Across the board, women's attitude towards happiness is measured on having it all and achieving work/life balance. Interestingly however, in a study conducted by Citi and LinkedIn, 36% of women felt marriage (perhaps the most important relationship we will choose to help us in that work/life balance) was not a necessary component inside *having it all.*

Our economy is a woman's issue, as we stand at the center of our socio-economic infrastructure. Today, 40% of American households have women as the leading or *only* breadwinner. This **seems** to prove we're more empowered than ever before. After all, we vote more than men do, graduate college at higher rates, and make up over half of the nation's workforce. Yet, according to McKinsey research, only a meager 26% of women are in top tier corporate positions. Although young women are earning more than their male counterparts are, this fact is only true for those who are single, childless, and live in metropolitan areas. These are the real, un-glorified, bare-bones statistics. As catchy publicity distracts us into thinking women are the new breadwinners of the country, the truth is women barely have enough money to buy bread. Before celebrating the She-economy, let's pull back the curtain a little further. According to *The American Community Survey of 2011*, of the *Breadwinner Moms* whom increasingly make up a larger and larger portion of our economy, one in four are single mothers. Their median income of $23,000 is sadly, not even half of what a typical two-parent home produces. More alarming still, 29% of those *Breadwinners Moms* do not hold steady employment. Who do you think is supporting these women? We all are, because these families cannot survive without government assistance. More importantly, who do you think cares most about these issues? I would venture to say it's women.

The difference between an independent male, and interdependent female, lies within our biology. A man's physical body is not necessary to raise children. Their overall investment in producing one life is not as high as that of a woman's. Whereas men can conceive with several different women many times over their lifetime, or even in a single month if they so choose, women must wait another nine months to have the opportunity to conceive again. Not only do women spend a considerable amount of their time and body's resources to form a child during pregnancy, we literally risk our life delivering them. The investment of our own human capital is high, as is obvious throughout our nation where there is a disproportionate amount of single mothers raising their children (without assistance from their co-parent) in comparison to men.

Whether we like to recognize it or not, we're increasingly becoming a divided nation; in no small measure reflected in the polarization of the poor and uneducated vs. the rich and privileged. Calling men our oppressors is a cheap shot when women comprise half of the population—yet hold only 18% of the female vote in Congress. It's noticeably evident: women do not vote for women. Can you imagine what would happen if women became more conscious consumers? If instead of watching shows that had women compete against one another, we followed intelligent discussions about social causes? The most powerful women of our nation go under attack each day and the argument against them is not an intellectual one. It's personal. Bullets are peppered with comments about their looks, proper feminine conduct, children, relationships, and more. Let's just say it, empowered women aren't called empowered or liberated, on the contrary, they are called bossy bitches. Women positioned in the spotlight are vulnerable to attack.

The true triple threat in our American culture is an assertive, attractive, and ambitious woman. The most obvious example of this was in the 2008 election when Sen. Hillary Clinton and Gov. Sarah Palin finally gave mothers strong political role models to applaud. It was an opportunity to witness how our gender could lead our nation into meaningful debates. But the negative attacks on their feminine characteristics only exacerbated sexism. As the perspectives of the young and bright develop, what do you think little girls will want to aspire to when society is more preoccupied with candidates' appearance than their leadership abilities?

Every interaction we have either brings us together or pulls us apart. When women fire attacks on one another, we encourage boys and men to do the same. Sensationalism is separating us all. To have men respect and support women, we must first respect and support ourselves. If we don't come together and use the purchasing power that is coming out of our pockets and into the pockets of decision-makers, **the *imbalance* will continue.**

Boundaries in the Workplace and the Double Bind

As our families live further apart, our workplace has taken on a greater role in our personal lives. The boundaries of employer and employee are changing because our need for collaboration has evolved to make room for the work-life balance. We cannot afford to separate our home selves from our work selves. People are not cogs in a machine. Micromanaging employees, because we do not trust they have the company's interest in mind, dismantles cohesiveness. Auditing employees' minute-by-minute may save dollars on the clock, but the tension of distrust has an adverse effect on loyalty and interdependence.

Chasers often are criticized for their lack of boundaries and sense of entitlement inside the workplace. Isn't this sense of professionalism (or lack thereof) not also indicative of progress? Our fathers played the role of the good ol' boys for years before our mothers (with their linebacker shoulder pads) muscled through male-dominated fields, so we might one day have a voice. Today we do. Arrogantly we lift winning trophies above our heads to flaunt our accomplishments. Bear in mind, we must be careful not to disrespect those who enabled our success in the first place. Our accomplishments are as much ours as they are of our support teams. We don't accomplish anything in isolation; nothing is truly done alone. Trophies tarnish. *Sharing* our victories enables our life to uplift those that surround us.

Businesswomen are a powerful force. As opinion leaders, our perspectives matter. In 2010, a group of researchers from MIT & Carnegie Mellon University, and Union College published a study in which people were grouped and analyzed to determine *collective intelligence*. As it turns out, groups that had a higher proportion of women were more effective, more sensitive to input, and more capable for compromise. Overall, these groups were better at decision-making than those groups who lacked a proportionate amount of women. For decades, women have wanted the clout that men take for granted, and today both genders are negotiating our leadership, work, and household roles for the better.

Women have become bolder and more assertive and men have adopted a more holistic leadership style. A report published last year by the Stanford Graduate School of Business concluded that women who are assertive (a trait that is often thought of as masculine) but who are able to turn these traits on and off depending on the situation, get more promotions than either men or other women who don't demonstrate such supreme duality. The study pacifies the intolerance afflicted upon women in business: the double bind. That is, if women behave in too feminine of a way, they won't be seen as leaders; but if they behave in too masculine of a way, they won't be liked. Typically, leadership is defined in masculine terms; feminine behaviors aren't associated with competitiveness or governance. When businesswomen learn to trust their natural leadership, brute force or authority is replaced by conscientious listening and communicating.

I used to think acting like a stereotypical woman was a liability. My inability to morph my small frame into a towering presence translated into a distressing Napoleonic complex. To be on equal footing with men, I de-feminized myself, downplaying my maternal nature and upping my competitiveness. Always on-guard, I tried to embody the commanding respect of a general ready to take on a good battle. Speaking with a chip on the shoulder, my demeanor carried authority in its tone and confidence in its speak. There was no apologizing for brashness. In those days, formal professionalism overrode a friendly smile. Denying elements of my identity to be more competitive with men left me feeling disingenuous. Whoever identified with Solange back then was, in fact, connecting to the fabrication of who I *thought* I had to be in order to achieve respect. Ingrained in me was the notion that success came by pretending to be tough like men and delaying love and motherhood for as long as possible. To be a strong woman, we must express both the male and feminine-like traits that made our personalities distinct and are fully our own.

When I did not feel *man enough* to compete in the business world, my overcompensation became self-denial. Expressing emotions of affection and appreciation, I thought, made me seem too flirtatious or weak; what some may judge as being too Polly Anna is a reflection of a flawed perception, not a truthful testimony. You are in charge of *your*

actions and feelings, no one else's. Denying our true nature, for the benefit of others, only transverses the boundaries of our authentic self. There's no need to apologize for who we are. If I am one of those over-affectionate, peppy people, so be it. We are not responsible for other people's opinions. We need always to remember this psychological boundary. Having someone disrespect or take advantage of our kind natures is a mark of their character, not ours.

Today, choosing not to alter oneself in defense against attack or criticism is a risk worth taking if you wish to feel more connected to what best defines you. The principles of love and humanity are the rules of life. Like our left and right cerebral hemispheres, a society needs both masculine and feminine modalities for our culture to evolve. The lines of male and female communication are finally melding into one: a more empathetic leadership style. Leading and managing employees with a nurturing perspective and open heart will help you consider not only the singular employee, but the family to which they are attached. Doing so will motivate and empower your employees to maintain a healthy work-life balance. Many studies note that having a comprehensive view of our workmates, as complete human beings (with lives outside of work) can be more rewarding to co-workers than higher salaries and bonus incentives. It is also more beneficial for the company as a whole.

After examining over 1 million employees in the highest performing work-teams, the Gallup Press found in its 2012 meta-analysis research that two driving forces in enabling a company's high performance are the following: a) knowing what is expected and b) accommodating, understanding managers. These elements are a discipline to respecting the contribution of our partnerships. More than ever before, with online reviews of company culture, management, and employment authentic collaboration has become a core business practice. Fear, jealousy, and competitiveness would have us act against our humanistic nature, yet they all stem from our basic need to defend and protect love. Perhaps in the workplace we don't call it love. Fine, change the wording... call it an immutable high-regard for those with whom you work closest. The economics of our country have forced us to a tipping point where we must choose to either continue endorsing the disparity between men and women or become more mindful consumers and vote for change.

Code of Silence

Women's self-concept is derived from the group to which we feel we belong. When we feel like the not good enough minority, we begin to second-guess our value and self-worth. We begin to compete (oftentimes against our own sex) to fit in with the higher status males. In our wanting to hang with the boys, many of us have felt the need to grow a second and third layer of tough skin so we can put up with demeaning jokes and appear less sensitive. The hidden message here is that men can be who they are, and women should adjust to their nature. This has caused women to deny our need for closeness (as we want to be more independent), sexual intimacy (as we want to seem sexually liberated), and even motherhood (as we don't want children to hold us back from promotions).

To understand why women would feel a need to dissociate from their feminine identities, Deborah Tannen, a linguistics professor and researcher at Georgetown University writes, "If women's and men's styles are shown to be different, it is usually women who are told to change." Men have been seen as the standard, since at the onset of the industrial age men contributed most (in terms of brawn and work hours) to our economy. In her book, *You Just Don't Understand,* Tannen goes on to say, "...and it is only a short step—maybe an inevitable one—from different to worse."

As far back as WWII, when Rosie the Riveter became the role model for women, our relationships with men and consequently other women began to change because **we** began to change. Working women needed to embody Rosie's strong, stern, and masculine character. It was a time of challenge for many families. Core values, traditional identities, and the need for self-actualization of women were tested.

These pioneers had tremendous pressure to prove themselves and their performance. They worked twice as hard as men, ignored derogatory comments, did their best to learn quickly, and de-feminized themselves, all so we could one day be accepted and **respected** in the workplace. The idealization of empowerment excluded our predispositions for relationships. In essence, here is when love became a social stigma as it stood in the way of independence.

Although our efforts have paid off in many ways, we have more stress and depression than any other generation ever before us. Our over-compensation at trying to become what *we should be* rather than *who we are* has left us with a feeling of inadequacy. In trying to balance it all, we remain too busy to relax and enjoy life; constantly over-compensating and always trying to prove we are as good as, or better than men are, rivaling them instead of trying to evolve together. We struggle with the same questions of generations past: is it selfish to want an identity outside of the home? Am I a good enough wife, mother, and friend if I take time away from them for myself? Women are expected to be perpetually available to their bosses, boyfriends, and children— at a moment's notice. It is crucial that we live inspired lives. To connect, love, and become fully realized is our right as human beings.

Women are relational human beings. We compare ourselves to others to have a better understanding of who we are and what we stand for. Judging others identifies and evaluates our own value systems, while distinguishing the most desirable social group or clique— reinforcing once again a social order. The foundation of our sisterhood is predicated on a code of conduct.

- We must be attractive, but never acknowledge it—doing so could make us seem vain.

- We should be smart, but not speak up too much, as this might decrease men's attraction to us. This loss of sex appeal consequently makes us less attractive to our social clique.

- Girl Power of the nineties instructed us to be confident, but being assertive also puts us at risk of being characterized as bossy.

- Above all, we're told to remain sweet and avoid expressing anger lest we be deemed difficult.

In other words, the code of conduct is a code of silence; a contract we've made with ourselves to exchange the female mind for a position seemly to that of men's. To do so we barter our intelligent, strong, and assertive voices for glamour, fame, and beauty. When we're consistently told we cannot speak our mind and assert who we are, we turn against one another and then inevitably against ourselves. Silence alienates us and impedes the growth of authentic relationships that allow for feelings of anger, resentment, and hurt in productive ways. Unresolved feelings are then released in covert and manipulative ways such as gossiping, name-calling, and discriminating against members of our own sex.

Side-by-Side

The greatest battle for our generation of women is a personal one: we struggle to liberate ourselves from our own excessive self-reliance and perceived stereotypes. As high achieving and ambitious as women have now become, we're still unable to appreciate our worth and ask for what we deserve. Christina Hoff Sommers says it best, "The opposite of male dominance is not female dominance, it's mutuality." Our grandmothers and mothers didn't have as many opportunities as we have today, and likewise, they were less stressed and happier people. The explanation lies in the division of labor: men and women used to work together. Traditional breadwinner and homemaker roles may have been too confined to the sexes, but at least they complimented each other. Our mothers may not have fully embodied self-actualized women in their longing for professional careers, however, a sense of cooperation still existed between men and women. Today, what stands in the way of the honoring of our full potential is a lack of inter-dependency.

We cannot have it all if we're doing it all alone. Young female rising stars shouldn't leave promising career paths and men shouldn't have to miss their daughter's dance recitals to try to find balance. This only leads us to look back on our lives and realize that in an effort to *have it all* we *missed* it all. We missed the opportunity to be the best version of ourselves in work and in life. The good news is, we can still make change possible by starting right now! We are the mothers of the next generation. We're ready to start listening and communicating effectively.

Women in particular continue to put the needs of others before our own and mommy-guilt now is as pervasive as it ever was. To have what's most important, we must get over our need to be it all. The answer is not to lessen our potential or to fit everyone else's demands, instead it's to extend the invitation to work together. American culture still seems uncomfortable with the notion that men take on occupations, which were traditionally seen as feminine such as teaching, nursing, and the home. Sadly, these occupations need men to balance our traditional ways of educating and nurturing in the same way as male-oriented professions benefit greatly by our influence.

As a society, we understand the role of a stay-at-home parent is important, but we feel uncomfortable watching our men take on front seat in the home. We see this emasculation in comedies and sitcoms when men are portrayed as weak, whiners who have bigger tantrums than their children do when they take on a more prominent role in the home. So we must ask ourselves, are women taking on more than we have to, not just because it is truly expected of us, but because we also don't want to see our men in a light that falls short of the strong, commanding personas? What does *man up* mean to you? Does it mean get involved in the home more or does it mean toughening up, working harder, and bring home the bigger paycheck?

Unfortunately, we still don't know how successfully to negotiate. Women feel selfish and men feel inadequate when we ask for more flexibility at work. We remain shackled by stereotypical expectations and our desire to remain in good standing. We don't have to be ardent feminists but we do need to speak up and be heard, and empower both women **and** men to be active participants in the home and workplace. Committing to equality for both sexes, aside from gender stereotypes, will allow us to grow in partnership. Let's strive to pave the way for our daughters and sons to have it all together, side-by-side. To reach our potential in work and in life, we must be honest and learn to navigate the high demands we all have with our partners and our workplaces. Our economy cannot afford to lose out on talented, professional women and our homes cannot afford to miss out on having conscientious men who help raise strong confident sons and daughters. If we're not creating flexible schedules, more affordable childcare options, and an equal balance of power in the home, then there's still a lot of work to be done in the work-life divide.

Take Marissa Mayer, president and CEO of Yahoo!, for example. As the youngest of women in the Fortune 500 CEOs (33 years old), she shocked the nation—and no doubt board members—when she announced her pregnancy the day of her hiring. Free speech was exercised loudly in our nation as career women and stay-at-home moms opined on Mayer's decision to take a two-week maternity leave and then build a nursery next to her office to work longer hours and still see her son. Over-achieving workaholic mothers, at last, had found their super hero. On the flipside, Marissa disappointed many of her fans by disallowing her employees to work from home. Despite a subsequent announcement of an extension of parental leave for both mothers and fathers, some still felt Marissa's executive decision to deny telecommuting limited parenting choices. It still appeared vying for promotions meant leaving parenthood hidden.

Given a choice between work and family, women chose their children and sacrificed personal growth in fulfilling careers. They started cutting back and not gunning for the more demanding positions. Rather than turning our backs on leadership positions, setting boundaries and frameworks allows us to give more of ourselves to our families and our work team without walking away depleted. Those who work a full-time job and come home to full-time household duties find it difficult to connect in authentic ways in either place.

Family-friendly initiatives at work bring stronger connections and contributions. When we create opportunities for working parents to be more available to their children, we increase morale and decrease turnover. Employees are more productive, loyal, and committed to their work environments.

The much-needed conversation about mindfulness has begun and it's extending well beyond personal choices on family/work/life balance. "To say, 'You can do it all and should do it all,' and not to get the support to me is frustrating," said First Lady Michelle Obama who in her own words has been in the shoes of many working mothers who struggle to maintain the balance act. "[I] know the challenges of leading a busy life at work and at home, trying to do a good job at both—and always feeling like you're not quite living up to either—and trying not to pit one against the other, really trying to balance.... I call myself a 120-percenter. If I'm not doing any job at 120 percent, I think I'm failing. So, if you're trying to do that at home and at work, you find it very difficult and stressful and frustrating."

To alleviate these issues The White House is standing behind the National Science Foundation (NSF) Career Life Balance Initiative, a 10-year plan to increase work-flexibility to parents in research careers. Some of their initiatives include delaying funding of research grants and fellowships for a year (to care for children) and funding for interim assistants to aid in the continued research efforts upon their absence.

The new frontier for both men and women is bringing families to work and work to our families.

Baby Elephant in the Room

Hindsight is 20/20. A few years ago, before I became a mother, I interviewed a candidate who had a compelling resume. She seemed hard working, client-focused, and managerial. What the resume did not have was information about her family planning. When she walked through the door pregnant, it was hard for me to understand why she would come in and take up her time and mine. She wasn't about to deliver, but she was well past the stage where we stop wondering if it's not just a few extra pounds. I didn't know how to address the baby elephant in the room. Not having anticipated this situation, I hadn't familiarized myself with the fair employment laws. We were at a standstill. She fidgeted trying to cover her belly and I tried to divert my eyes not to expose her. Neither of us spoke honestly and it all was very silly. An extra twenty minutes were spent (delaying the entire work day's schedule) making idle chit-chat just to make her feel more comfortable. Since she excluded any details of her plan of action post-birth, I built my own assumptions. I assumed she would have to take time off and take care of her newborn. The thought that her husband may have had the flexibility to help her, honestly, never crossed my mind. He could have been the stay-at-home parent for all I knew, but that concept was even more foreign.

Investing training dollars on someone who could potentially quit in the near future did not seem like a smart business choice. My aesthetic clinic was too small to constitute having a daycare program. In hindsight, there was a daycare center three doors down, which could've been something possibly to work out, had she been the right fit, for the position in the clinic. Unfortunately, we didn't conduct a thorough interview to find out. Small businesses are often short on cash flow and there aren't substantive tax breaks to constitute the rising costs of childcare as a benefit to employees. The interview, nonetheless, deserved an honest conversation in trying to negotiate family-friendly options. As I said, I hadn't yet experienced mommy-work-guilt. Our perspective changes as we move from single entrepreneurs to working mothers and having experienced it all for myself, that interview would probably been handled very differently today.

It's important to note that our nation stands behind most industrialized countries in maternity and child-care laws. The only family leave available to Americans is a three-month maternity leave and covers only about half the labor force. There is a lack of paid sick days, tax breaks for businesses to offer daycare options, and disproportional wages for part-time work. The reality is that many working parents have to forgo much needed pay in order to stay home with sick children. The economic downturn of 2009 brought with it a man-cession. Men lost their jobs at a higher rate than women did. Leaving the work place to tend for babies at home was no longer a viable option for mothers. A two-income household was necessary in the recession. If we're ever to see our economy bounce back and hold the workforce at a comparable standard with those countries we judge ourselves against, then we must accept our share of the responsibility and move forward with practical answers.

Recently, the FAMILY Act or the Family and Medical Insurance Leave Act, has proposed a national effort to help fund up to 12 weeks of paid leave each year to qualifying workers for the birth or adoption of a new child, the serious illness of an immediate family member, or an employee's own medical condition. The United States is the only industrialized nation not to offer paid maternity leave. As a result, the Human Rights Watch has condemned the US of human rights violations. Employees could potentially collect benefits equal to 66 percent of their monthly wages, with a capped monthly maximum of $1,000 per week.

From Business to Babies

When I finally became pregnant I didn't resume my workaholic tendencies, instead my mind went blank. It was as if the dark of night had fallen and the peaceful sounds of chirping crickets lulled my mind to rest. This preggo serenity was lovely, enlightening even, but it wasn't *me*. My Type A personality morphed into this new Mother Earth, albeit lazy persona. I sat outside reading spiritual and philosophical books, watched Eckhart Tolle on the web, and rubbed my belly with coconut oil for hours. However, as I rubbed that ever-expanding belly in the hot days of summer, something else was happening, my brain was shrinking. Again, not metaphorical jargon, it was literally decreasing in weight. Not some rare disease either. This new state of bliss wasn't a spiritual awakening; it was the product of progesterone and estrogen hormones being pumped into my body like a factory on high. Much like a horse tranquilizer, their effect of decreasing stress is so potent that for about six short-lived months I ignored all facets of my business and lived without a care in the world. This sedation is our bodies' way of preparing us for the plunge into motherhood, bringing focus on the fetus and away from our lofty ambitions.

Don't be alarmed. Although this is a natural state of affairs in pregnancy, our brains do go back to their original size six months after the little brain bandits are taken out of our bodies. The only problem is our mind has been rewired for more stress and a primal worry to protect our kin.

During pregnancy my brain's neuro-chemistry was in as much control of my actions and therefore, subconscious mind. I now understood that the voice in my head, commenting and assessing my every move, was simply trying to carve out a self-concept: I am this and not that, I deserve these things, and I shouldn't be doing those things. This self-concept, often called the Ego, can be our greatest friend and foe. How well we view our own performance against our expectations determines whether our Ego will encourage or deprecate our spirit. Our self-concept changes when we become mothers, as does our confidence level in our new role. The idea of what *type* of mother we will be is created by our society, home, and personal ideals.

As wonderful and illuminating as this existential awakening was, I had not arrived at Nirvana's front door after labor. The hippie-woo-woo-granola *me* eventually came out of the trance, stopped meditating under a tree, and began seriously questioning what exactly comprised my identity. Between Clomid's apathy, Eckhart's philosophical *enlightenment*, and my business sense returning full force, I decided to delve deeper into investigating why *having it all* was so important. Why had I striven so fervently to become excessively self-reliant and successful?

CHAPTER 5

Eve's New Apple

"Instead, Eve was made interdependent, of him, but not him. Birthed from his rib, from under his arm, Eve was to be protected, and from that which guards over the heart so she may bring Love."

-Solange Jazayeri

*W*oman, it is said, was created for Adam's companionship. Not made as his superior or inferior, Eve was of Adam's center; neither from his head to rule over him, nor from his feet so she could be tread over. The trinity of civil rights, sexual revolution, and women's liberation movements planted us at the base of the tree of knowledge. As the serpent gave Eve the pill to swallow, her eyes widened and her vision of a new world became clear. She demanded sexual and intellectual equality, not realizing that as long as Adam remained the standard, she'd always feel less than and ashamed. Embarrassed by her vulnerability and exposed insecurities, she covered her natural self.

Our culture would like to have us believe that we value our service to men more than our service to society as a whole. Portrayed as seductresses at best and cheap replications of men at worst, it's as though women are destined to remain in the Garden of Eden. Men and women are creation's perfect design; much like puzzle pieces, we are made to complete one another. Yet, we've chosen to de-feminize women and haggle the female mind for the status and admiration of men, thus denying the very thing that makes our gender saintly: emotional interconnection.

The Revolutionary Tribe

Experiencing emotional interconnection is the foundation for much of a woman's self-concept. Historically, tribal women have been the hearth keepers. Our Darwinian wiring has made our mindsets both supportive and competitive as a way to protect the clan. We value the tribe's future over the individual—that's how newborn babies are kept alive. We are genetically predisposed to depend on one another for care so naturally we take on others' emotional needs above our own. The whole world's conflicts therefore become our inner struggles.

Revolutionary women challenge our primitive, protective natures because they threaten social norms. Rebels are valiant, courageous, and usually a bit delusional. Their inner voices are louder than the crowd is—despite society's attempts to drown them out. Revolutionary women are evolutionary. They don't conform to the world; they ask the world to conform to them. These women propel the feminine identity forward. Some battles are won, some are lost, but by and large, **evolutionary** women are heard.

Contraception becoming mainstream made our independence a tempting proposition. Those who wanted to evolve to higher levels of satisfaction now had the chance to do so both personally and professionally without the fear of pregnancy getting in their way. However, this also meant women would have to contend with their personal decisions publicly. This new sect of women threatened the social norm. Instead of rallying for one another, we began to rival each other: the selfless vs. the selfish, the pull out and pray vs. the pill poppers, the homebound mother vs. the newly freed feminist. Motherhood is an assumption in the lives of women. Certainly, we will not all become biological mothers, but mothering by vocation or friendship is in our nature. People in general, expect women to bear children and care for others. When we don't, our character is questioned as being too self-absorbed. Damned if you do, damned if you don't! The modern woman replaces the ageless quest "To be or not to be?" with "To bear or not to bear." It's as if the answer to this question determines the type of woman we will be, what shoes we'll step into each morning.

Cat Fighting

Let's take a step back here to recognize the social uprising that ensued when feminists took out their megaphones. Their intention was to be evocative and radical, and perhaps they *had* to be to be heard or paid attention to. Many people felt personally offended when feminists began speaking out. Women were asked to choose a side and defend their position tooth and nail, and in doing so, female empowerment became greater than our personal choices. Anyone who did not agree with the idea of liberating women—getting us out of the home—was deemed an adversary and thus, our solidarity was dismantled.

When we roar, we stop communicating... more importantly we stop listening to our internal voices. Nevertheless, we still run into anger on the pathway to deeper meaning in our lives. Anger is a powerful emotion—it consoles defeat, and sparks passion when it feels like you have nothing more to give. This in-group fighting phenomenon gave women the opportunity to break free from inferiority. A new social hierarchy was created which ranked the good, better, and best women. In a sense, this system was meant to break through the glass ceiling of oppression. However, the jagged edges of glass have cut us with self-denial and discrimination. This sorority-group-think became marred by shame tactics, turning our benevolent natures into cattiness. Spitefulness can temporarily normalize our fears of insufficiency. Professor Brene Brown, a well-known expert on guilt and shame articulates that, "...research tells us that we judge people in areas where we're vulnerable to shame, especially picking folks who are doing worse than we're doing." Although women fighting against one another was loud and explosive, at the core it was truly a personal conflict. It was an inner battle turned outward. Defaming mothers lowered the status of others, for momentary relief from personal inadequacies. This normalizing strategy always works against us in the end. Dishonoring someone else lowers our integrity while increasing our self-hatred.

Before the pill, there was one social norm for women, and now women could gain status outside the home. However, at what cost? Women who were going after their dream professions were defamed as *selfish* libertarians who didn't care about traditional family values. In essence, women raising children became *just* moms. The pill changed the topography of our environment. We couldn't un-see the new world. There were new opportunities, but there was also heart-wrenching introspection. The question of the day became, ***"What type of women are you?"*** Friendships were dismantled when labels, categories, and hierarchies came to be.

A vicious cycle ensues when we all go on the defensive side. Parenting is extremely personal. You can call me ugly, mean, and stupid, but call me a bad parent, and my bright red nails will extend and scratch. A hiss may be involved as well. This is true for most mothers. Having our parenting skills or approach questioned or judged taps the jugular, and when we humiliate someone else, it makes it easier for us to bring that judgment into our life. At the end of the day judgment, in any form, makes us feel inherently two-faced.

The Faces of Eve

I once took an acting role with a script called the *Three Faces of Eve*. It was based on the real-life case of a woman diagnosed with multiple personality disorder known today as Dissociative Identity Disorder (DID). After a traumatic event in childhood, Eve's personality was split in two: Eve White, the dutiful, humble wife and mother, and Eve Black, an adventure-seeking, risk-averse, free spirit. Finding the thread, which weaves all our *selves* together, can sometimes be hard. DID is not common, but it does resemble the dilemma we as women face in trying to consolidate our work selves, friend selves, dating selves, into one cute, neat little package. All the milestones in our lives building a profession, having children, becoming lovers, split our personalities, into differences of dress and behavior. Society is okay with us being sexy, smart, and motherly – but not all of those things at the same time. Through extensive psychotherapy, Eve developed a third personality named Jane, presumably to consolidate all three identities into a more complete persona. Sewing our fragmented pieces completes the picture of who we are.

I love clothes. I mean *really* love clothes. This little obsession goes well beyond the normal girly magazine-trending-retail-therapy type of fix. Fashion is one of the greatest loves in my life. Clothes allow us to reflect, enhance, or wallow in the moods we are in; comforting our broken hearts in the warm cave of oversized fleece sweaters, builds confidence for the little black dresses. Clothes wrap us into characters. More than one style magazine has perpetuated the power of a great pair of shoes, purse, and designer glasses. Apparently, if you have all three, nothing else matters. According to the experts, these fashion statements can make the difference between looking like you rolled out of bed hung over, or looking like a cool, chic, bohemian rock star. As women, we're familiar with hiding problem areas, or perhaps better said, covering up our imperfections by highlighting our assets. The choices we make in clothing affect our attitudes. They're designed to be protective security blankets to build confidence inside our business personas, yoga practice, mommy culture, etc. When we say, "This outfit doesn't feel like me," what we mean to say is, "This 'identity' does not reflect the 'personality' I wish to convey." Imagine a Buddhist nun wearing Versace glasses, six-inch stilettos, and a Fendi purse. Her credibility would be instantly scrutinized.

Sometimes we forget we're animals, and much like bulls who become enraged by a red cape, our brains and subconscious are complex, and hard to fully control. To illustrate how our character can be ignited by our dress, consider the studies conducted between 2007 and 2008 at the University of British Columbia. After tracking 600 participants, it demonstrated that participants who were exposed to red before beginning minute, meticulous tasks involving things like memory retrieval (test-taking) and proofreading, performed thirty-one percent better than those people who were exposed to the color blue. Moreover, researchers have found that when wearing red, people react with greater haste and more forcefully than to any other color. Transversely, those people who wore or were exposed to blue, excelled in creative activities and were more likely to think outside of the box. It seems a little ridiculous, I know, but the fact is, our clothing (what we wear and how we perceive ourselves inside them) actually has an effect on the way we behave.

Cultural norms have a strong impact on what we deem appropriate. For example, in South Florida where there is a large Hispanic culture, short, tight, and skimpy is not incongruous with being a mother or being a professional. In fact, sex appeal is celebrated. Any given day or hour, you can turn on the Spanish TV channels and see scantily dressed women broadcasting the news, acting in soap operas, or putting on an apron longer than their mini skirt, to share with you their new guacamole dip. Channel surf to more Americanized channels and women are portrayed in a much different manner—newscasters, reality TV celebrities, talk show hosts, all have distinctly different styles. Likewise, this is seen throughout our country. Different storylines come to mind when we imagine a Southern Girl, a City Girl, and an East Coast Surfer.

Putting on clothes allows us to reflect, enhance, or wallow in our moods. An extension of our personalities, our clothing tells a story wherever we go. I change outfits with the same frequency pageant girls change wardrobe in a 2-hour segment, to accommodate for the roles I jump into throughout the day. Both style and personality can either express or mask our inner being. Each garment and amulet gives clues about our identity. Style can be as much a meme for an identity as personality is a meme for our authentic nature. A meme is a symbol, which tells a story quickly. It is not the complete story of who we are. For example, a wedding ring to signify commitment, a tie-dye shirt to symbolize a free peaceful spirit. Like our naked bodies, our inner being is what lies underneath what we choose to show off.

Stepping into New Shoes

We select our shoes with precision by first mentally mapping out where we'll be, how long we'll be standing, and how fast we'll have to run from here to there, to everywhere. The perfect outfit equates to perfect image. Nevertheless, multi-tasking what we wear is as complicated as multi-tasking our roles; it rarely works. How I wish there were a pair of shoes with the comfort of flip-flops, sexiness of red stilettos, and bounciness of running shoes. Alas, shoes can't be everything either. Business suits are not designed to clean up quickly after a little spit up and high-heeled shoes are not designed for days at the park.

I made the foolish decision one day to jump from lunch date to get-up back into mommy mode without first adjusting the differing needs in footwear. Looking inappropriately dressed to be at a school function, I ran clicking from side to side on the pavement until coming to an abrupt stop as the cement changed into grass. Isadora's school was celebrating Arbor Day at the park (a holiday centered around planting trees) and here I was wearing high-heeled stilettos, a pencil skirt, and a top which very much needed a suit jacket to look halfway decent. The rest of the afternoon was spent carefully placing my long black hair in front of my chest trying to cover it up. Modesty is not my greatest asset, a trait that comes under much scrutiny amongst women.

Mothers and teachers laughed as the heels of my shoes left a trail of indentations on the green for the procession to follow. Each gawky, graceless, sinking step churned and aerated the grass. It's a shame they didn't capitalize on the opportunity these perfect holes provided for gardening and planting. The scene only got worse when a heavy shovel (much taller than my daughter and about my weight) was handed over to start digging. Florida's blazing sun trapped its heat in each strand of my thick black hair, matting it against my now sweaty torso like a semi-absorbent mop on a wet surface.

Isadora was so excited. Anxious to be planting her first tree, she was completely unaware I was now cemented into the ground by a batter of fast-drying mud clumped around my four-inch heels and a tight skirt, which bound my legs in place. Again, I repeat, modesty is not my best trait, but I am not immune to embarrassment. Ignoring the inappropriateness, I stepped out of the shoes, lifted up the skirt, and made room for the strength of my thighs. Tying my damp hair back, I began the Herculean shoveling. Shoveling while standing straight up was nearly impossible and despite my best efforts, my low-cut shirt was exposed. C'est La Vie.

The scorching sun stood over my shoulders, firing its rays like an angry father condemning his daughter's pin-up billboard of...glistening hooters! (Not my proudest moment) I could feel the prickly sensation of scorn and mortification on my face. Still, a perfectly well deserving tree needed to be planted by an equally well-deserving little girl, so the stares and judgment had to take a back seat. Isadora and I got down and dirty. When it was all over, she stood tall next to her erect tree. Wrinkled, smelly, and muddy, I did, too. Thankfully, I had disregarded the adults and focused squarely on my daughter. The tree would be there long after the whispers and stares. A little embarrassment never killed anyone.

True confidence is built in these instances, when instead of sheltering ourselves from criticism we choose to connect to something much more meaningful. Upholding our values rather than our image has us act with true integrity to allow courage to rise. Confidence doesn't come by wearing an attractive outfit and acting pristine, but by watching ourselves behave bravely, despite public scrutiny. When I looked into my daughter's big brown eyes, staring back at me with glee, the world melted away. My image didn't matter as much as this opportunity to be wholeheartedly there for her. Isadora didn't understand, nor care about a wardrobe malfunction, let alone my need to be proper. She doesn't think of me as *that* hoochie mom, she thinks of me as *her* mom. Getting our hands dirty and picking up the shovel to support those we love builds self-esteem for both parties; those we care about feel valued and in turn, we feel valuable.

Like it or not, we're judged by the way we look, and consequently our clothing is a large part of that. No one knows what others are thinking, and even if we did know, we can't control other people's thoughts. Sure, there may have been some parents with strong opinions; however, most were focused on their own kid and their own shovel. Looking at this scene, it is tempting to begin a long list of should have, could have, but didn't. Tempting or not, this kind of thinking is counterproductive. When we take into account the perspective of others, it's important that we evaluate who we entrust to give us proper feedback. Sometimes the most courageous thing we can do is step out of ourselves (and our embarrassment) to remember what we are all about.

Late Professor Abraham Maslow believed in seeking out moments of joy in our everyday. Peak moments, as he called them, are a time during which we are able to leave our self-conscious selves and integrate our being to the moment. As he said, those "people [who are] self-actualizing listen to their own voices, they take responsibility, they are honest, and they work hard. They find out who they are, not only in terms of their mission in life, but also in terms of the way their feet hurt when they wear such and such a pair of shoes and whether they do or do not like eggplant or stay up all night if they drink too much beer."

The outside world doesn't have a complete picture of who we are, where we come from, what we value, or how it is we wish to connect to those we love. When I made the decision to step out of my shoes and into my daughter's, I recited this PEAK acronym adapted from Prof. Maslow's advice in seeking out peak moments: Purposely Engage in Acceptance and Kindness. The purpose was to connect with my daughter, not impress others. Engagement meant trying not to mind map what others were thinking of me, but instead in the digging, and of course, in the fun I could be having. Unable to run home and change, accepting the situation for what it was, and more importantly accepting that I am much more than this poor representation of a pious mother—allowed a kind laughter in. We sometimes need to remind ourselves not to take the moment (or ourselves) too seriously.

We all feel self-conscious at one time or another, but the staying power of our inner critic relies on the stories we feed it. I could have chosen to step into the shoes of my perceived critics at the park, but for one thing, they may not have even existed, and for another, adjusting my actions for their benefit could have prevented this peak moment with my daughter from happening. Earlier that day (on the date with my husband), I had felt beautiful. The revealing shirt and eye-catching skirt had captured Nick's attention. When his admiring eyes looked at me, I glowed. That was my peak moment with him. Now, at the park, my glow had the hue of an amber lamp at the red light district. I had not changed (neither had the outfit) but the backdrop of the story had made me *feel* vulnerable to judgment.

Much like Eve, our personalities split when we become mothers. We're expected to be asexual around our children, but be sexy wives to our partners. Unlike men, women are asked to change personas several times a day without a nuance of other roles. If, by chance, one of those personalities is spotted at the wrong place and at the wrong time we feel labeled and judged. Work life, mom life, and sex life don't like to share boundaries.

Those Type of People

Given the fact that we mostly behave in automatic ways, it's important to understand how the description we hear from others about ourselves (strange, pretty, funny, etc.) help form our self-concept. In Carol Dweck's book *Mindset,* she shares her extensive research in uncovering how outside influences, from parents to teachers to coaches, affect our ways of thinking, particularly, the labels which affect our self-esteem. In *Mindset*, Dweck makes the distinction between fixed and growth mindsets. Growth-minded individuals find intrinsic rewards from personal evolution. They understand the labels surrounding their personalities are like book titles and headlines, which give us an idea of the subject. To know more we must read on. Someone who seems to be a musical genius may have a proclivity towards music, but virtuosity is the result of a committed practice—not simply luck.

Taking the book analogy one step further, as we delve deeper into our psyche, we find a library of books written by our families, friends, and society. Very rarely are we privy to all sides of a story. More time is spent describing the successes than the journey it takes to get there. Pride can turn a factual story into a hyperbole, elevating the wins and minimizing the losses. When we are typecast into a character, we can find ourselves stuck in the expectations of others, which brings us to the fixed mindset.

Those who have a fixed view of themselves believe in the fate of their character's constraints, i.e. the limit of their intelligence, physical strength, type of personality etc. Labels, whether positive or negative, can be damaging to their self-esteem if we don't see a way out of the roles we feel we are supposed to play. For example, if we see ourselves as career-minded and ambitious it can be hard to disappoint our mentors when we decline a promotion to stay home and take care of our children. The personality trait of ambition evolves to mean something entirely different in home life. A woman doesn't change after children; she evolves a new side of herself. Whenever we are not able to meet the high expectations and high standards of others (and ourselves), it is encouraging to remind ourselves we're always in transition, always trying to do our best.

On the one hand labels can be liberating, for example, those diagnosed with attention deficit disorder often times feel relieved to put a name to their struggles. Knowing there are therapies to counteract such a condition can help us become more self-compassionate as we evolve away from the label (or learn to live within its boundaries). On the other hand, when labels create prejudgement or stereotype schemas, we go into an *I-already-know-that* mode of thinking and close ourselves off to new insight. Those labels can also constrain us into a fixed mindset: *I'm-not-like-that* thinking that shuts down an opportunity for deeper introspection and growth. Allowing ourselves to be typecasted into this or that type of woman; whether that be just a mom, working mom, or hoochie mama; disavows our true feminine natures, which are far more complex.

Although we reject the notion of being labeled and stereotyped, we all inherently do it. We have to because it's how the library of our minds sorts out endless amounts of information. Categorizing helps us access the knowledge more readily. Our virtues are expressed differently in us all. A growth mindset is important to our psychological development as it motivates us to stand up for our core values and remain committed when forced to make tough decisions. Life is about compromises and sooner or later, we come to realize there are no types.

In a study of 1,200 Millennials across the nation, 96% of those interviewed believed they will do something great in their lifetime, and 76% said they were highly motivated to serve society. We are so concerned in **becoming** somebody, we forget that we are already someone. Each day we're born and reborn in the minds of strangers. In our interaction, an imprint is left behind as to what people that look and behave like us are like. When we are true to ourselves—acting with self-integrity and kindness—we model that authenticity for others. Self–actualized people know what they stand for and do not compromise their beliefs for the gratification of the moment. Every moment, every interaction is an opportunity to practice peace. If you want to impact the world, be authentic in every interaction. We have an influence on those around us. Our reputation derived from our everyday roles expands well beyond comprehension.

Think of the last time you were on vacation. How did you describe the type of people there? How many people did you actually meet? Do you feel that was an accurate sampling? Now imagine if one of those people had done something out of the ordinary—good or bad, would your description of the culture be influenced by the behavior of this one person? Now imagine the amount of people you come across in a week. Surely a few of those are strangers and unbeknownst to you,

you have become the character representative of your town, your community, your family, your last name.

You and I are *those type of people*.

CHAPTER 6

Being Discovered

"I believe in the power and mystery of naming things. Language has the capacity to transform our cells, rearrange our learned patterns of behavior, and redirect our thinking."

– Eve Ensler (poet, activist, and playwright)

*A*s we make faultfinders our playwrights, the tone and cantor of their words narrate our internal scripts. In previous chapters, we've discussed competition and the perils of allowing others access to our unconscious habits. In this chapter, we begin the work; deconstructing and disempowering negative narratives to habituate more productive patterns of thought.

As outlined in the introduction, The Phenomenal Four (derived from our neurobiology) mold our perceptions and basic temperaments. These neural networks are responsible for our personality styles. They are also what I refer to as Reservoir Cats, that posse of inner critics inside our minds who give voice to our ego, or better said, our self-delusion since this mental state destabilizes our authentic self from feeling in harmony.

To review, these particularly formidable systems are:

1) *serotonin* that influences Rosie the Riveter's protective moral nature

2) *dopamine/related norepinephrine* which energizes Wonder Woman's adventurous style

3) ***testosterone*** drives Ms. Bossy's competitive ambition

4) ***estrogen/oxytocin*** (with larger doses expressed in women) account for Ms. Homemaker's mama bear instinct

The ego is self-centered. It seeks to create an identity apart from others, yet it seeks to be loved. To prove we are worthy of such love, the ego constantly tries to assert its specialness. This is the delusion— as it separates us from our humanity where we understand we are all deserving of unconditional love and respect (our self included). When we don't get what we want, or feel insignificant in the eyes of others, it is the ego who cowards away or lashes out, teeter tottering from entitled thinking to rationalizing why we aren't good enough.

Words are powerful. They are memes that allow us to categorize, summarize, and describe a shared language. Each of us has a set of words that are particularly good at cutting deep into our psyches and activating our emotional hot buttons. For instance, the word *intelligence* is loaded with myriad subtleties and meanings in relation to personal experiences and perceptions. Since I can remember, the family joke has been that I live in outer space. Absent-minded is what my family calls it. This is not entirely incorrect since I contemplate the mysteries of the cosmos more frequently than most, but in youth, I translated this description to mean brainless bimbo. Intelligence, I believed, was central to a person's self-worth (a view I no longer hold). Naturally, not wanting to be cast with this pet name outside of my inner circle, I've spent much of my adulthood modulating an effort to overcome, yet not overcompensate for the observed handicap. Until the moment we choose to fixate on our distinctions, they are not handicaps. There are inherent rewards to all personality traits, conventional or not. Our perception of the cultural characteristic is what affects us. Harvard Professor Howard Gardner theorizes there are multiple intelligences summarizing them as visual/spatial, verbal/linguistic, logical/mathematical, body/kinesthetic, musical, interpersonal, intrapersonal, naturalist. Absent-mindedness isn't a defect in personality, it is simply a word categorized wrongly. Lack of linear thinking is closely related to creativity and there are several advantages to dreaminess. My ego was perhaps stuck in this one description, this one meme I had created of what intelligence meant to me. The ego tried its best to prove I am not *really* smart, or *that* great, or *that* talented, so to not identify with a word that will disappoint me later. This self-denial often took the form of rationalization.

Typical *"**it's not me, it's you**"* type dialogue whenever a compliment was received:

Compliment: "You're so smart"

"[It's not me.] You're so nice"—deflected praise

Compliment: "Great, job!"

"[It's not me.] You just don't know the *real story*"—minimizing praise

Compliment: "You're talented"

"[I'm not talented.] You don't see, it was just luck "—rationalizing praise

When I couldn't deny, deflect, or discount someone else's favorable opinion, I simply turned against them with a rationalization like "***You*** must not be ***that*** smart yourself to see me for what I really am." This phrase is hard and embarrassing to admit, but if someone's opinion of my intelligence was too high, then my opinion of them lessened. It's a fact that everyone is better than or smarter than someone else at something. Therefore, I too must be smarter than others at ***some*** things. Not recognizing the eight different facets of intelligence that develop at different phases makes us rank ourselves amongst peers. My fear of not being smart enough gave the Reservoir Cats ample room to defend and critique my intelligence.

'Pretty or Smart?'

It was the end of finals week at college when some friends and I decided to ignore our need for sleep one more night. We celebrated by gossiping about teachers and poking fun at classmates over bottomless pitchers of beer. A tiny box of index cards was our main conversation starter (all we needed to engage in a public forum debate). A card was pulled out which posed a very interesting question, "Which would you prefer: to have an I.Q. score 10 points higher or to be 10 points more attractive?" The stipulation: an I.Q. score of 10 points higher would inversely decrease your level of attractiveness by the same measure (or vice versa).

We had only a moment to think before giving a response. My immediate thought was, "Smarter. I'd much rather spend less time preparing—or in this case studying—for life and more time living it." That answer didn't bid well with the group, and my assumptions that brains would make life easier elevated the argument into an intellectuals' debate (i.e. twenty-somethings contemplating the greater questions of life between tequila shots). Thanks to having the Internet at our fingertips, a pros and cons list was quickly drawn up by the end of the night.

If 10 points more beautiful we could potentially:

- Receive faster promotions

- Higher salaries (average of $250,000 more in lifetime earnings)

- Leaner prison sentences (in general)

- Be perceived as more educated, funnier, and amiable all around

The winning consensus: choose beauty unless you've already secured a partner and a high-paying job. You may be smart, but if you don't have *the looks*, it's likely you'll have to work harder for the advantages above. From our rudimentary Smartphone research, a study conducted in Great Britain and the U.S. revealed that, on average, attractive men and women are 14 IQ points smarter.

The conversation now turned from the theoretical to the moral. The British researchers explained the denoted beauty advantage may have been the result of the coupling of smart men with more attractive women and their offspring inheriting desirable genes of both beauty and brains. Playing devil's advocate, I argued against the Darwinian Theory, choosing instead the *halo effect* argument. The halo effect is a psychological phenomenon where people take a particular trait like *she's pretty* or *nice* and apply it to other character traits like *she's also smart*. Teachers, in particular, are prone to falling into the halo's trap and therefore pay closer attention to those students who seem smarter. These students, in turn, receive the benefit of more attention and engagement, which translates to higher tested IQs. Not considering myself to be brilliant, or a super-model, I could appreciate what having a little extra attention could bring.

Long after the hangover of our drunken debate had worn off, the question lingered inside my brain. Once I'd started interviewing for jobs, almost every prospective employer, had at some point, addressed the issue of **my** appearance. Perhaps I wasn't the ugly duckling I'd always seen in the mirror. Men in the business world informed me that playing up attractiveness was an advantage in sales, while women warned against it. Not wanting to be seen as a naïve bimbo, I thanked these same women for their mentorship. However, those women who were true confidants whispered the real secret in my ear, which was that being an attractive woman could be used for or against you. *If you have it, flaunt it, but be coy. Never flaunt it in front of other women and never admit knowing your attractiveness to men.*

After a year in marketing and sales, I decided that having a M.B.A. would enhance my resume, making me more than just a pretty face. In trying to ditch the real world and gain confidence, I found myself paddling along, once again as the ugly duckling amongst highbrow swans in academia's pond. One class in particular was especially challenging to both my grade point average and self-esteem. A decade later, I cannot recall the subject material of the course. What I do remember, however, is the feeling of betrayal by my own. Throughout the semester, the class was divided into rivaling teams for mock business exercises. Team selection happened as rapidly as the pouring of balsamic vinegar into oil; little droplets of vinegar dispersing and finding their way to one another, huddling together before returning again to form one solid group. Suffice to say, I was not in the first-draft lineup. Despite there being only three girls in the class (myself included), my female comrades turned their backs on me. The more astute students in the class had their own elite clique, and so the more reserved group became the perfect match by default—too polite to kick me out. This rejection was new to me. I'd always been invited to group study sessions and college night outings, but inside winning team selections, choosing me was apparently seen as securing a loss or at the very least a court-side penalty. As self-deprecating as that sounds, it's simply a fact. My grade set the curve's (bottom) standard and the other students knew I was in jeopardy of failing the course.

Despite the war-like dynamics of the class, the professor was very jolly. He acted and looked like Richard Dreyfus dressed up like the Florida Santa Claus: the spitting image of those postcards with Santa donned in a Hawaiian shirt making sand-angels on the beach. He was kind enough to stay after class and provide extra help. Being in my early twenties, I felt our bond was like that between a grandfather and granddaughter. As tough and competitive as my classmates were, it was nice to have a professor who took me seriously. I don't know if Mr. Claus had unintentionally placed a little halo above my head, but I appreciated the extra tutoring. His review of my failed test questions during after-class tutoring provided an advantage to knowing the topics likely to be on the next exam.

By the end of the semester, I had only one test and paper remaining. I'd studied so much that my grades and self-confidence reflected the effort and I had greatly improved. On the last day of class, I waited with baited breath as one person after another received their test scores and then left. I was last on the list. With my heart pounding Samoan drumbeats in my ears, slowly, Prof. Claus handed the paper over. I'd passed the class! Elated, I thanked him profusely, expressing my tremendous gratitude for his extra time and effort with me. Giving him a friendly hug, I said a final goodbye. He seemed touched by the sentiment, so much so that he reciprocated by touching my tush. The slow beat of the Samoan drums shifted to the sound of silence after a DJ record comes to a screeching halt... I was stunned. Silenced with shame. Just as quickly as my confidence had seen fireworks, now its weak smoke trail plummeted downwards in humiliation. Like a branded cow, the heated imprint of his hand disheartened my spirit.

The jury of critics, my Reservoir Cats, began weighing in: *"It's my fault. I hugged him."* —Ms. Boss *"Does it really matter? It's not a big deal."* —Ms. Bunny.

The semester was over. The final grade rested in his hands as silencing insurance. Friends had already teased me about being the Teacher's Pet, so saying anything about the incident would surely prove my Bimbo-ness. They could have even thought I brought it onto myself. Prior to that point, he'd never been flirtatious; I'd thought his doting was grandfatherly. Now, I felt like a schoolgirl in a suspiciously short uniform. *"Collateral damage."* –said Ms. Bossy. *"It may have just been a playful football-pat-on-the-bum."* –Ms. Bunny retorted. In addition, if I'm honest, Ms. Bossy affirmed with a tone of false-empowerment: *"Well, he got his cheap thrill. I secured the B. Even exchange. After all, it wasn't corporal punishment; he didn't slap me with a ruler."*

Because the action wasn't overly salacious, it ate at my self-respect like a termite—a threat to my home. In hindsight, there had been some heebie-jeebies moments when The Reservoir Cats had sent out a warning... I had talked myself out of the improper glances though, and instead, reasoned it was all in my head. Looking back at the scenario with thirty-something-year-old eyes, I see things much differently. A man is a man. College girls are appealing—even to older men. Dirty Santa wasn't all bad. He did help me, encourage me even, but it didn't change the fact that his conduct was unprofessional and inappropriate and the incident was humiliating. Years later, I turned the whole scene into a joke and laughed it off with friends, but that walk of shame out of the lecture hall wasn't at all funny, no matter how I may have tried to minimize it years later. In the long walk to the car and drive home, Ms. Bossy had the final word, *"He **gave** me that grade, I'm not that smart."* Insecurities had come full circle. In that space, at that moment, I became my psychic nemesis, the dumb absent-minded pretty girl. The Bimbo in sheep's clothing had been uncovered.

Despite knowing the stereotype, when the stigma is applied it stings and its poison spreads. That Bimbo the M.B.A. was supposed to discredit lived on. I tried to convince myself it wasn't that bad: *"It was done in a playful manner"*—Ms. Bunny. Not to mention, (again) he was much older. I pardoned his actions, instead of categorizing it and calling it what it was: improper. The crux of this story is that improprieties may seemingly broadside us, but we must be attentive to our own minimizing dialogue. Our inner voice is our guardian. Learning to differentiate between harmful chatter and wise advice helps us hone in to the respect we all deserve from ourselves.

Had I chosen to listen to that knowing inner voice, that intuition at the onset of those early days of uncomfortable feelings, I wouldn't have said goodbye with outstretched arms and a warm embrace; his touch, my boundary. Taking responsibility for his impropriety and blaming myself crossed my own psychological limit. It takes two to tango and I had accepted the preferential treatment, but I wasn't responsible for his misconduct. The breach of trust with that professor was a violation, but dishonoring my own integrity was an act of self-cruelty. I have to ask myself, had this happened to a friend, had she come to me asking for guidance and compassion, the 'It's not a big deal' dialogue wouldn't have been heard.

Choosing to listen to the criticism of our inner voices, rather than our support systems, weakens our self-concept. Shame enters, as the betrayal of trust affects the trust we hold for ourselves. As it turns out, that woman's advice whispered in my ear proved to be true. Being an attractive woman can be used for or against you but be careful how that influence is used; seemingly, short-term gains can undermine longer term benefits.

You Eyeballing Me?

As humanity evolved, so did the language centers of our brain. Conscience needed a way to relate its intentions, and so words became the conduits to do just that. Therefore, words and specifically the *integrity* of our words are the most important covenant to our personal evolution. Each of us holds a unique perception given our distinct upbringing and genetic makeup; therefore, although we may share the same language, we do not always share the same meaning.

Despite all the reality shows and boot camps that shame us down like drill sergeants—yelling out 'love yourself more,' the truth is, for the most part, we do love ourselves. Most of us appreciate our character traits. Our guilt and discomfort come from not recognizing what it is we most value in ourselves. Ellen Langer, Ph.D. and her student Loralyn Thompson had a hypothesis: they believed that each personality trait that has a negative connotation is linked to a positive correlate. Furthermore, this relationship between negative/positive is the reason why changing behavior is so hard.

To test their theory, Langer and Thompson asked participants to identify character traits they had tried to change in themselves. The list given had words such as grim, gullible, rigid, etc. (adjectives usually thought of as undesirable). They then received a second list of positive words and were asked to rate how closely these words described their personalities. What participants did not know was that both lists were essentially the same list. The only difference was the connotation each word carried. For example, *gullible* in one list was *trusting* in the other. Their hypothesis proved to be right. Those individuals, who had the hardest time changing their habits, felt the most proud of the positive traits in their personality attached to the undesirable behavior.

So, how do words uncover our core values? Helen Fisher, Ph.D. configured a word-type study, evaluating a list of 170 words among 178,532 participants to determine how people describe themselves and the qualities they seek in long-term relationships. Remember the Phenomenal Four? Fisher argues that Explorers, Builders, Negotiators, and Directors, are influenced not only by the environment, but also by their inherited neuro-pairing. These key players are Dopamine (Explorers), Serotonin (Builders), Testosterone (Directors), and Estrogen (Negotiators). We have *all* these neurochemicals, but the degree to which our unique cocktail is mixed determines our personality's value system.

Each personality style has its own culture, comprised of behaviors, values, and language. "I'm a word purist," a good friend said to me recently. I, on the other hand, can't truly understand the significance of a word unless I hear it in a sentence and know who said it. We all see through our own kaleidoscope of color. My world has many colors all jumbled up together. My friend's primary red is my maroon - a blend of red brown, orange, and pink. Therefore, judging people on intention rather than on delivery levels the field. We don't all share the same lexicon or communication style.

The table below highlights key words and challenges for each personality style.

Personality	10 Key Words	Challenges
Ms. Wonder (Explorers)- The pioneers of the tribe. They are optimistic, creative, goal-oriented, assertive, and greatly motivated by curiosity and achievement. * Secondary traits add to this personality type.	adventure, venture, spontaneity/ spontaneous, energy, new, fun, traveling, outgoing, passion, and active	Autonomy- not bound by schedules or punctuality Disorderly has been linked to dopamine. Elevated dopamine activity has been found to increase addictive behaviors, i.e. gambling, alcohol abuse, etc.
Ms. Rosie (Builders)- The protectors of the tribe. They have high moral standards, are reliable and patient in nature. Leading disciplined lives, they focus on detail and are orderly factual linear thinkers.	family, honesty, caring, moral/ morals, respect, loyal, trust, values, loving, and trustworthy	Disciplined- need structure to feel comfortable. Repetition can raise serotonin, (decreasing anxiety), which may be the reason why this type likes to keep a routine in place. Linear– their step-by-step approach to life can sometimes cloud the nuances of seeing the big picture. Factual- what is vague can raise suspicion High Moral Standards- Can give guilt a special place in Builders' lives as they try their best to abide by society's standards of propriety rather than individual desires.
Ms. Homemaker (Negotiators)- The romantic hippies who uphold peace. Harmonious relationships are possible because they have the ability to hold two opposing views in their mind as different perspectives rather than contradictory. They are also the most agreeable of the other types and most willing to make personal concessions to make everyone happy. Highly sociable and empathetic, they are able to see themselves in others. Negotiators are also very introspective.	Passion, passionate, real, heart, kind/ kindness, sensitive, read/reader, sweet, learning/ learn, random, and empathetic/ empathy	Romanticism can lead Negotiators to be idealists and too trusting, feeling deeply let down when they witness inhumanity. Agreeableness challenges self-sacrificing. Highly Empathetic individuals have shown to have more mirror-neurons, giving their minds the ability to mimic what they see in the outside world within their minds. Making the pain, embarrassment, and sadness their own, which may keep Negotiators from asserting their own feelings and boundaries if they believe this may cause pain in others. Introspection can make this type very self-aware and at times self-critical of the idealized notions they evaluate themselves against.
Ms. Bossy (Directors)- The stoic heroes who lead with quick decisive action, but they are not emotionally impulsive. They are analysts. Their Autonomy, independence, and success ranks high for these types as they seek to take care of their responsibilities. They have narrowly focused but intense interests. They are non-judgmental & systematic in their thinking, able to focus on the problem at hand without outside noise.	Intelligent/ intelligence, intellectual, debate, geek, nerd/nerdy, ambition, driven, politics, challenge/ challenging, real	Autonomy- Directors can separate themselves from the crowd. They have few close friends. Placing their agenda as winning or be better than others can turn inward to self-criticism. Systemizing- Directors can get frustrated if they perceive there's a waste of time or resources. They like to get to the point (of fact-finding) even at the cost of appearing blunt and impolite. Logical- struggle with the ability to mind map others' emotions making them less empathetic. * Documentation shows the link between aggression and testosterone in competitive natures -- to become alpha males and females. * women with high levels of testosterone are more likely to enter male dominant industries and to delay (or opt-out) of marriage and have less children, abuse, etc.

Impostor Syndrome

The fear that we may be exposed as not being good enough (i.e. to debunk stereotypes) or that our mistakes may have a negative effect on others (i.e. maintaining the stereotypes) stand as internal barriers to fully expressing our unique gifts and talents. Dr. Valerie Young describes this psychological trap of *exposure fear* as the Impostor Syndrome. In Young's words, impostors have a "…persistent belief in their lack of intelligence, skills, or competence. They are convinced that other people's praise and recognition of their accomplishments is undeserved, chalking up their achievements to chance, charm, connections, and other external factors." In laymen's terms, impostors feel like frauds on the verge of exposure. Young believes these inadequacies are associated with knowledge or skills and are most prevalent inside academic and professional arenas.

Criticism can feel like the *uncloaking* of the sheepskin, which can even bring momentary relief. How often do we give more merit to our faultfinders than we do our champions? When a real life critic came into my life to bash me, I was somewhat thankful the charade of *being smart* (when I really wasn't) was discovered. My promise to the critic's harsh feedback was "I'll *be* better," not "I'll *do* better." This subtlety is smart but important. *Be* and *do* constitute different memes/paradigms in our minds.

Impostors don't necessarily have low self-esteem. On the contrary, they may be confident in their skill sets in many different arenas; it's the anxiety women feel at being discovered as substandard or not good enough at a given task that is the problem. This Impostor Syndrome begs the question: how often do our preconceptions on *paper,* about our ability to achieve and show success, limit us?

"Being good at math is an important part of who I am." This was the self-selecting statement psychology professor Shen Zhang and her team used to segregate 182 undergraduate students in the spring of 2011 within a mass survey. One group (sample A) was told that convergent thinking between sexes had been found in mathematics. A proctor explained that the new pilot study was to examine these convergent and divergent ways of thinking. Students were then asked to write their names, date, and gender on the front cover of a test booklet and continue writing their name on subsequent pages. Sample group B was told that due to coding and confidentiality their booklets had to be assigned an alias name (Jacob Tyler, Scott Lyons, Jessica Peterson, and Kaitlyn Woods) to be written on all the pages. Men and women scored the same on the mathematics test... as long as women acted under an alias name. Regardless of the assigned name—male or female—when the female students didn't have to write their own name on the test, their mathematics scores were on par with their male counterparts.

The amount of stress female subjects often go through to prove themselves, to appear adequate, has made many choose anti-anxiety pills over conscious self-care. So why did the male participants not experience such influential anxiety? One reason was men viewed this test as an examination of their arithmetic skills only. Men often credit their wins on their innate abilities and blame their losses on the difficulty of the task. In contrast, women (more often than not) minimize our wins and write them off as a cause of external factors. The losses, however, are more readily accepted and internalized as confirmation and mark of failure. This further ingrains our mental schemes that we are just *not good enough*.

The higher women rated their mathematical ability as a part of who they were, the worse they performed. Not obtaining a good enough score put their self-concept in jeopardy. When we view ourselves as the underdog in a testing situation, the resulting scores don't just measure how capable we are at completing a task, they also measure how *good* we are, period. When placing under a microscope and testing a women's reputation and competence, female subjects were testing their perception of self-worth and thereby experienced a *stereotype, or self-reputation* threat.

On a larger scale, there are three bigger, more pervasive problems underneath the surface of non-anonymous testing. First, women often base their own self-concept on the group to which they belong. We evaluate ourselves in comparing ourselves to our peers. In a recent study, when Asian Americans were primed to acknowledge their ethnicity, they performed better in a quantitative test (presumably because of the stereotype that Asians are better at math), however, when participants were reminded of their female gender their performance declined. If women feel like outliers, it seems they're more likely to second-guess whether they are worthy of belonging, and in return, feelings of not being good enough rise. Second, when women feel they're a representative of a group (especially a minority group), they are more likely to stress about the effect their decisions will have on the community around them or not being good enough for others. In other words, women worry more about the whole rather than just the individual. Therefore, their fear of not being enough has greater implications; it's not merely their reputation at stake. They are also concerned with how well they're able to take care of the group they care about. Finally, men and women internalize success or failure differently. When men succeed, they often attribute their victories to their skills. It is of no consequence whether the task at hand is easy or hard. As previously mentioned, when they fail, men often blame the error or misstep on the high-level of difficulty of the given task. Women on the other hand, credit their achievements to external reasons such as the ease of the task, luck, or charm—while internalizing the failures as evidence of their insufficiency.

An Altered Mind

Mindfully classifying and cataloguing our inner dialog can help normalize our emotions. Although we cannot change our autonomic subconscious thinking, we can alter the labels we attach to our activities and censor the dialog of self-doubt. Removing these blockages will promote a smoother path to our self-actualization. Our ego believes in limited resources; instincts tell us there is a finite amount of money, men, and opportunities available, but the competition is fierce. Our humanity, on the other hand, believes in abundance, that when we are hungry and alone, we can transcend beyond our humanness to an existential realm. Choosing to opt out of scarcity and into abundance is how our authentic voice comes to be heard.

We tell ourselves our happiness rests in changing who we are, and our situation. We'll be better with our New Year's resolutions, with our goal setting, with our new jobs. Why are we so discouraged when at the end of the day, week, or year we've reverted to our default setting? We understand what our intentions are, so why is it so hard to change our behaviors? Once we can release the cloak of perfectionism, we are better able to integrate our intentions to our actions so we may exercise our growth mindset.

CHAPTER 7

Imperfections

"Love is what is left when you have let go of all the things you love"
Swami J (Swami Jnaneshvara Bharati)

*O*ur truest, forlorn love is perfectionism. We're convinced that perfect lovers, wives, and mothers can hold everything in place and keep everyone happy. Worshiping its gravitational pull like that of the sun, we place perfectionism at the center of our careers, marriage, and family. Like Don Juan and his ego, the deity of perfection doesn't show up as a liar, it shows up like Prince Charming bearing gifts of admiration and achievements. His magnetism resting on a game of hard-to-get, the closer we come, the quicker it escapes our grasp. Soon we realize that no one is perfect and words like *special* and *extraordinary* are not reserved for an elite class.

We know it is unrealistic to have and be it all *all* of the time, yet we still find ourselves striving for the impossible. Researching this backwards thinking led the research to the Type E* personality. Harriet Braiker, Ph.D. was the first to introduce the term to catalogue women who had an insatiable need to prove themselves through accomplishments and people pleasing. Constantly overextending themselves, Type E*'s place the scoreboard of their self-worth on meeting the expectations and satisfaction of others—perfectly.

Type E* Chasers compare themselves against the best mom, best boss, and best friend, ignoring the sacrifices they had to make in order to be the best at any one category. Instead, look at idols in their totality and recognize that *balancing it all* is a learned practice and not a stagnant reality. When the illusion of the ego fades and we acknowledge our fallibility, our most private thoughts, desires, and fears, come to be known and we receive from others what we all need most: understanding and encouragement.

Symphony No. 5

It was love-at-first-sight in a college bar. Nick was a month away from graduating dental school and I was two weeks away from making a decision whether to study fashion in London. I decided that, given our infatuation with one another, the fashion program would have to wait one semester to see where our relationship would lead. At the time, putting love before my passion for fashion seemed like a sound decision. As the following semester came and went, our love only intensified. Instead of delaying my study abroad program, I changed my course of study. Bye, bye fashion. Hello Nick and a happily ever after...or so I thought.

It's easy to give up on the mirages of our career dreams when our relationships are so real in comparison. *It was a small concession,* I thought. Small decisions however, lead us to the larger more life altering choices. Therefore, it happens that throughout our lives we sacrifice our passions to be in good standing with people we admire and love—only to find ourselves resentful years later.

Our courtship wasn't easy. If people have internal anthems, mine is *Beethoven's Symphony 5 (Da da da da...da da da da).* There are light melodies to my personality, but most people experience the arduous, passionate, and turbulent tones. Oh, how I wish I could remain in the playfully romantic parts of the composition, like the whimsical clarinet—light and sweet! But inevitably, I always go back to the dramatic crescendos. I'm certain that Nick's mother only heard the dramatic part of my symphony because from the moment we met, she wanted me gone. As I walked into her calm and quaint Greek restaurant, the windows shattered with the force of my brass section. My blaring trumpets scared her. In contrast to my demeanor, there's not an ounce of commotion in her son; he's consistently quiet and steady. From that point onward, my life became My Big Fat Greek Wedding...minus the comedy.

It was apparent from the start that if I wanted a future with Nick, I would have to find a way to win over his parents. This was not easy. They had their hearts set on him marrying a nice Greek girl (not a loud, obnoxious Spanish one). My in-laws are an old-fashioned and discreet couple. I am amorous and affectionate. Melting our cultures together took a lot of finessing. Nevertheless, in the end, Nick was a package deal (well, we're all package deals). Having a good partnership with him meant having a good relationship with his tribe. I was convinced that once his parents got to really know me, they'd see my love and admiration for their son and we'd all hold hands together and sing Kumbaya. The only thing they had to do was give me a chance.

Nick wanted to build a dental practice near his parents and I was not going to be the floozy that broke the family apart. So, I moved to the small town with a large billboard that reads "Welcome to Destin, the world's luckiest fishing village." The white sandy beaches of this vacation town would be great for his profession, but detrimental to mine. His long-lashed brown eyes won my heart and the independent persona I held on to so strongly got weak in the knees. I made the decision to change—not only my location but also whatever needed to be changed in me for his love and commitment. By the way, the childhood lies about what matters most: the titles, the last name on our wedding day, and the zeroes and commas in our paycheck, had come full circle. This lie asked that I gamble my career ambitions for acceptance into Nick's family and his professional potential.

Although our family is very close now, it was a journey with many painful moments. There was a time when I looked at the beautiful man I'd married and recognized I had made him my entire world and he simply was not enough for *me*. I had moved away from my family, friends, a career in fashion I had fantasized about since childhood, and now stood alone and apart from all the things and people I loved. This was two years after Nick had promised we would move if I didn't like Destin. Moreover, two years later, I had neither friends nor a ring on my finger to have my move seem worthwhile. However, by then, I also was so utterly in love that staying together was less painful than being apart.

As ambitious young Chasers, we lived between worlds; orbiting in the dark amidst our family, and what is best for our future family. This is perhaps why as women it feels as though falling in love and loving our professions is a zero-sum game.

As young women we're conditioned to look at our relationships and give rank to the career choice that appears to be the most established and most financially prosperous. It seems pretentious to ask our partners to compromise their higher salaries to accommodate our professional growth. Yet, the compromise of what's best for the future of the relationship, has the partnership grow to its highest potential.

Relationships aren't always going to stay in balance; there must be open dialogue as to what each individual needs to evolve personally and therefore, as a unit. Self-sacrificing to pretend to be a *perfect match* makes us impostors. Short–term discomfort (i.e. becoming vulnerable to rejection) can bring long-term trust when two people find ways to give away little of bits of what they love, to honor the bigger love they share together. Relationships are about negotiating our passions with our partners to build a unified vision. *Not* to do so undermines the partnership, and the weight of each other becomes too unbearable to carry.

Where did the Romance Go?

Little by little, we give up what we love for the sake of love, but falling in love is not about giving up ourselves. It is not about being the perfect match. It's about allowing our partners to bring out sides of us that are worth knowing and exploring. Relationships serve as reflections to our identity and a complement to our temperaments. We're infatuated with one another, because not only do we find each other irresistible, but also because their love for us makes us evaluate how we see ourselves. For instance, *if I think he is great and he thinks I am great, well then that must mean I **am** great.* We try mentally to *mind map* our partners, in essence, using them as mirrors to see ourselves. Altering ourselves solely for their benefit can cause us to misidentify ourselves. This change confuses attraction, since more often than not, the very thing which makes us attractive to our partners, can also be frustrating to them. As we change ourselves, our partners see us differently and we see ourselves differently as well. We become melancholic and disenchanted when our partners no longer bring out positive feelings in us and we blame them, when in reality we are who altered ourselves.

Let's say you are a naturally generous person. Your partner loves how you always consider his perspective, many times doing things he loves to do for the sake of making him happy and being together. As a rule, you're very giving of yourself and your time. This same trait you extend to your work in the community. With time, he begins to ask that you not be so charitable (towards others). He, unlike you, is a bit more pragmatic with his wallet and leisure time. "Think of yourself first," he says. "Your charity work is taking away from our family time and resources." After you hear it enough times, you begin to agree. Maybe your volunteerism can take up a big chunk of your weekly activities. It is hard for you to say no when non-profits are in need of help. Rather than having to say *no,* or disappoint your fellow volunteers by not committing as much time as before, you decide to bow out gracefully, excuse yourself from said charity and focus entirely on your partner.

It is common for generous women to feel taken advantage of when others need their help. This volunteer dilemma is common; we want to give our time and self, but too many withdrawals of time and money can have us turn our backs on community service altogether. However, the activities that support our personalities, in this case charity work to support generosity are important elements to our identities. Although it may be true that time and resources take away from the romantic relationship, it is also true that charity work connects your humanity. So naturally, when the focus turns entirely to your partner you begin to ask more from the relationship. You try to have him fill the void that is left when your emotional bank account is no longer being filled by your altruism outside of the home.

As you change your behavior (what your partner found endearing about you in the first place) and start becoming more self-focused, you *both* find yourself in a new quandary. Your partner no longer appreciates the advice he once so readily gave you, since the very personality trait (altruism) that had brought you close in the beginning has been altered. Your partner doesn't look at you in the same way and you no longer feel great about yourself in his presence. Long story short, it's a lose-lose situation whenever we alter ourselves for what we believe our partner wants us to be. First discover who you innately are through your core values. Find ways to protect these values [so you are able] to walk away from activities or relationships that ask you to give more of yourself than you are willing to give.

Often, it's not only our personalities we alter, but our minds can literally alter as well. Our brains marinate in some sort of hormonal love potion no. 9 during courtship. The intoxication fools our senses as we replace our lover's desire and expectations for our integrity. This is our ancestral hardwiring, which forces us to compromise and build up a partnership long enough for children to come out of infancy. It takes about three to four years after the wooing has passed for our brains to sober up. The higher order sections of our brain finally reactivate and we come to realize altering ourselves for the benefit of a single person hinders our personal evolution. No one person, profession, or thing can fill the void that befalls us when we give up all the things we love to attain the respect and admiration of a valuable something or someone. The investment is too high. Trying to maintain the happiness others have with us destabilizes our own sense of well-being. The more self-sacrificing we take on the higher and greater expectations we set (and consequently feel we must maintain). After the long stemmed roses wilt away and the hot, sizzling sex fizzles, we find ourselves asking: Is the reward worth the cost?

Romance or romantic attraction lessening can lead us to misread this next season of our relationship as a compatibility issue. Potential new partners begin to look more attractive and we question whether we are still in love. However, it is at this pinnacle point that we can create a much closer and more intimate relationship. Here we *chose* to stop looking for a perfect partner, or to *be* perfect for our partner. Instead, we chose to use the partnership to help us further develop integrity.

Love-mates are like helpmates that challenge our deepest held values through arguments, communication, and ultimately negotiations. Finding the best person may not be as important as being the best version of ourselves for another. Taking responsibility for our own emotions and self-development forces our ego to let go of its entitled mindset. Thus, we must be honest about our needs, without resenting another human being for the decisions we choose to make. Commitment is not just a piece of paper that legally binds us. Commitment is a practice in love; the return to one another again and again despite the ebb and flow of romantic feelings.

Seemingly afraid of putting others at the forefront or even alongside, women are delaying love and marriage to avoid sacrificing what's important in their lives at any given time. It's easier to fulfill our personal objectives without the pressure of having to make concessions for the benefit of those who rely on us. However, the problem lies not in loving others, but in the rotating of our lives around them, making them our center—without carving out a place for our own self-growth. Melding our lives with another person strengthens our humanity because our commitment is predicated on valuing something greater than our individual self values. Learning how to love others while also respecting our boundaries protects our authenticity as we learn to stand up for what we want and what we cannot live without. To do so, we have to stop trying to mind map other people as a way to evaluate our self-worth. Falling short of the expectations of others is an unpleasant fact.

Ultimately, we stand on our own, for even the sun bids us farewell at nightfall. Unless we are able to love and respect ourselves with the same amount of commitment we have given to those activities, which inspire us, and those whom we love, we will be left in our solitude, contemplating how we'll manage to continue until daybreak. Building a life with a partner requires that we know ourselves so well that we are never lost in one another. If the sun never shines again, we can build our own fire for warmth and live off our inner light for guidance.

Super Women

"Trust me, super-women have super stress," late Dr. Braiker warned. Her research recognized the tremendous pressure involved in striving to achieve financial and personal excellence. It is the chase of young and naïve romantics. We are so caught up in love that we forget to breathe and eat. Our idolization takes all of our attention, and we lose sight of self-care.

Braiker concluded that our culture was suffering from an epidemic of perfectionism. Nearly three decades after Super Mom became a popular ideal, not much has changed. Women still struggle to establish personal boundaries in both love and in work. After interviewing, studying, and counseling hundreds of women, Braiker concluded that although women felt more independent than ever before, their independence had come at the cost of anxiety and debilitating stress.

Pretending that we can handle it all, Type E*s and now Chasers, try to keep embarrassment and shame at bay, by doing it all themselves and giving up sleep, personal hobbies, and play in order to do so. Making comments like, "I can handle it, I'll find a way" limits others from helping us. There's an exchange that takes place when problems and solutions are communal. Truthfulness makes others active participants in sharing the load of life's emotional stresses.

Their influence and perspective bonds us as we learn the value of interdependent relationships over our self-centered view of excessive self-reliance.

When we want to be everything to everybody, we give up a sense of identity to gain social acceptance. After interviewing hundreds of women, Braiker found that those women who did *have it all* still felt restless and unsatisfied. Women still have to maintain their success, and their expectations and the expectations others have of them didn't level out once they met the goals, they only increased. Loving ourselves unconditionally requires that we let go of this perilous romance with perfectionism and carve out a self from the things and people we love.

Good Enough is Not Enough

Before having my children, I thought angels would sing in the background, playing little harps as we breastfed and transcended to maternal heaven. Not true. There are no angels, just painful nipples. Five years ago, our first daughter, Isadora, was born prematurely. The career-minded persona I had, suddenly shifted into a mother with new roles to balance and master. This tiny, frail infant illuminated my greatest fear: failing to rise up to the challenge of motherhood. Personal achievement and hard work was no longer measured in the same way. There was a new language and culture to learn. Failing to be a good mother was not an option. Besides, I didn't want to simply be a good mother, my child deserved *the best* mother and nothing short of that!

I vowed my family would get a different woman than I'd previously been. This woman would be calm, structured, and joyful every day; not the high-strung and stressed out workaholic. She would never turn on the T.V., she would make organic baby purees, and wear lipstick to accentuate her dazzling, happy smile. I could not sustain this Super Mom image and my self-concept crumbled at her feet. Breastfeeding alone was frustrating—having to sit there instead of being productive. Moreover, when I was able to go to work and be productive, the mommy guilt felt all-consuming—I should have been able to sit there with my daughter. I felt pulled in every direction, a personal catfight with competing identities and different agendas ensued.

Mommy Homemaker wanted to be 100% devoted to our baby and domestic life.

Wonder Woman could be in three places at once.

Rosie the Riveter bellowed, "Do it! I can do it!"

The Boss felt underperformance at work was unacceptable.

In addition, **Bunny**, well, overnight the intimacy in the marital bed was adjusted to accommodate for a crying baby. *Adjusted* being code for *went away* and Bunny was quick to point out stress was not sexy.

These harsh critics were devoid of self-compassion. Every critique had a story embedded within its own set of belief systems handed down from family and culture. Trying desperately to become the perfect mother while still holding onto a shred of independence, I tried to find balance by cutting back work to part-time. Despite this, my work had now quadrupled; I was now taking care of a home, a baby, a husband, and a business. Naively my attitude was *I can do it! Both here and there! Everywhere!* When there weren't enough hours in the day, I cut out sleep. When the baby fat didn't just magically melt away, I cut out deliciousness - you know, carbs, sugar, and bread, and replaced them with caffeine and celery sticks. That was a crazy time - no one can do it all alone. The guilt at my failing to measure up anywhere stomped over my confidence and self-respect.

Ms. Boss said: "You're not productive enough."
I replied, "I will cut out sleep. I will be better."

Ms. Bunny whined: "Not hot enough."
I consoled, "A marathon should help."

Ms. Mommy Homemaker shook her head side to side: "Not a good enough mother."

I shamefully answered: "Part time is not cutting it. I will sell the business and devote myself entirely to our home life."

Of course, I knew this was all illogical and extreme. However, punishing myself made me feel better. If I felt bad about it, I could at least minimize my guilt. Nevertheless, this tactic didn't quiet down the Cats. It only left me sleepy, with foot sores and leg cramps, and a ravenous desire for cheese and wine, lots of cheese and wine. As you can imagine, expressing my breast milk over the sink as not to get my baby drunk also failed at minimizing the mommy guilt. That type of guilt is its own special strain.

Desperate to find a better way, I began a four-step practice:

The first was to find space between these ridiculous characterizations so I could observe this automated criticism. This is where the idea of the Reservoir Cats originated. By labeling their negative dialogue I could recognize the language and tone, trap it inside a funny cartoon, and move on.

Second, I did not argue or rationalize with my self-criticism. Instead, I would say, (sometimes aloud) "stop" at others I would say, "I am, I am, I am." And let the mindless chatter subside. "I am" was a self-compassion tool, an abbreviation from the sentences: I am worthy. I am part of something holy and something greater than I am. I am deserving of kindness. If I said, "Stop" or "I am" aloud while my thoughts were in mid-sentence, it was easier to control unwarranted thoughts from developing. It took some practice. Meditating also was a great aid in exercising mind control. Meditation is not as much about quieting the mind (as that is nearly impossible) but of recognizing the voice in our mind as it arises. If we can allow our thoughts to pass by like clouds in the sky, we practice the art of letting go of the negative.

The third tactic was simply to move my body — physically move my attention elsewhere. Of course, exercise is always a great way to combat negativity, but so is getting in the car to buy groceries, taking a walk, or making funny faces with our children.

When the negative thoughts became repetitive, the final solution was to confront the Reservoir Cats head on (pun intended). These terrorizing bullies can be guides and mentors if instead of denying their criticism we ask deeper questions and thus, turn criticism to introspection.

Why, Ms. Boss? Is my being productive important? What will doing more prove about who I am?

What proof do I have, Ms. Bunny, that I'm not hot enough? Hot enough for whom? And although we all may have mommy guilt at one time or another, what if instead of trying to find proof that we aren't good enough mothers we directed our thoughts in detailing why our personalities are perfectly matched to the lessons our children need to evolve?

Feedback is a constructive response to a situation, a suggestion for improved behavior. Criticism on the other hand belittles us. It has no positive purpose or value. We must learn to control our inner dialogue, as we are who authorizes them. When emotions trigger, a neuro-chemical response is released. After 90-seconds, it will wear off and we are solely responsible for choosing to reactivate it or not. Guilt-inducing dialogue plucks us away from fully enjoying the moment. The curious thing is that while my ego battled itself inside these archetypes, not one of these idols encompassed what I really wanted for myself. Rather than denying our limitations and anxiety, we can choose to accept our feelings for what they are – feelings. Transient emotions.

Instead of trying to stifle the critics, I began to acknowledge they served a purpose in my life. Up to that moment, the high standards I'd set for myself had propelled me forward. I'd accomplished most of my personal goals, but now it was time to move past achievements to finding harmony with who I was. Not who I was to become or was working at becoming, but who I will *always* be. Being at peace with oneself requires that we see ourselves with kind compassion. Through this new interaction with my inner voice, I became more mindful of the broken record in my head laid in me by family, culture, and society. The demeaning self-talk was a way to protect myself from outside judgment. If I was hard on myself, that meant I had beat everyone else to the chase.

CHAPTER 8

Perfect Measurements

"Pretty women wonder where my secret lies, I'm not cute or built to suit a fashion model's size, But when I start to tell them, They think I'm telling lies, I say, It's in the reach of my arms, the span of my hips, The stride of my step, The curl of my lips, I'm a woman, Phenomenally, Phenomenal Woman, That's me...."

-Excerpt, Maya Angelou, *Phenomenal Woman*

*I*t's from our physicality that our identities come to be known—and we are phenomenal. We must safeguard the walls of our inner sanctum for it is there we exist. These sanctuaries we call *bodies* house the birthplace of our soul. Nourish the body as you would the most precious and sacred of beings because in you is where the remarkable intelligence of the human spirit thrives.

Size Matters

I've yet to meet a woman that hasn't twisted her torso to look down and count the dimples of cellulite on her squeezed butt cheeks. Have you ever done the wiggle-into-the-jean-jiggle? Slowly wiggling into a pair of jeans by shuffling hips side-to-side while holding your breath to suck into place an already small stomach (which no longer feels small) to close the tenuous top button. Stiff as a board, we then pat down a pooched-up diagonal zipper and cover the newly created muffin top with a long shirt. All of this we do to walk twenty steps into a restaurant, sit down, and immediately unbutton and unzip this torturous chamber underneath the security of a tablecloth's skirt. I hope this hasn't been the case and that you've been kinder to yourself than I've been. If there's a hell, it has to be living out eternity in a pair of tight, skinny jeans, two sizes too small.

Let's take a closer examination as to how media's negative messaging affects our food plates in the day-to-day and where our vanity, if left unattended, can lead us. This section's aim is to help you understand how eating is at the cornerstone of life; intimately connected to emotions, self-concept, and ultimately our relationships. Change the way you look at food and you can change your life's experience.

So many of us fall prey to our skinny histories. Practically every woman has a pair of jeans as a barometer—skinny, fat, or at least a little closer... Our bodies change with time and sometimes we forget that the ideal number we've named as *happy weight* was achieved at unhappy times with unhealthy diets. Choosing to fit into a pair of denims by any means possible (even if they're so old they're out of style) instead of fortifying physical and mental health, can deprive us of much more than calorie intake. Trust me; happiness does not come at a size 0. Think about that number for a second. Is it even a number on its own? This is not a philosophical question; just think about what 0 represents. Zero represents nothing. It's the number of invisibility. After children, more slack was needed to make room for new mama hips. For a girl who loves clothes and fashion, it was hard to move out of the invisible size. Adding a digit meant the elite zone of model-thin was now out of reach. I'm not a mathematician and maybe size 0 isn't immeasurable, after all, now there's a size double zero. As we have concluded, there is power in naming things and marketers know it. *Banana Republic* may have thought size 00 wasn't tiny enough or minimizing enough, so these are the following petite sizes they offer: 000, 00, 0, and then 2, 4, 6, etc. The triple 0 is just another example of America's obsession with thinness. By the way, what happened to the number 1? Women are attached to numbers and if a clothier's loyal customer base implies imitating model-like figures, then size 000 has real value.

It's worth repeating: Happiness certainly doesn't come in a size 000 either, especially if you're starving to get in it, or you're *just one stomach flu away from your goal weight.* Spain was the first to set a limitation on overly thin models and because of this stance other countries have. Among them, Israel and the Mecca of high fashion, Italy, have taken steps against clothiers promoting their brand with much-too-thin models. They recognize the danger in impressionable younger people trying to emulate their walking mannequins and have responded with legislation regulating that a model must sustain a B.M.I. of 18.5% for three months prior to working in a runway show or fashion shoot within the country. The law also maintains that advertisers must include a disclaimer, which indicates any Photoshop retouching used to manipulate any photo taken for commercial use. Qualifying the value of our bodies by how well we fit into an unrealistic standard disconnects us from our natural selves.

Changing the Standard

If it's true that hate is rooted in love, practically every woman I've ever known loves one body part more than any other on her body (or at least loves to hate it above the rest). Women of all shapes and sizes, thin and otherwise, walked through the doors of our aesthetic clinic to buy self-love or at least to minimize self-hate. Technologies inside medical spas are nothing short of amazing. Used alongside a healthy lifestyle regimen, non-invasive laser treatments can provide added support to our dieting efforts without having to go under the knife. Please note however, the operative word here is *healthy.*

Beautifully fit women would sit in the entrance hall of my clinic, envying the airbrushed women in magazines and waiting to duplicate those make-believe images into their very real life hips, bottoms, and thighs. All the while, they completely ignoring that the average fashion model in a magazine fits the anorexic benchmark nor reflecting on the team of stylists, makeup artists, and lighting crew, plus the added bonus of digital modification all used to sell a promise of perpetual beauty (inside a look that is far from natural). In this sense, gratuitous tabloid reading has a stronger effect on our unconscious, much more than many of us are aware. Any type of engagement that captures our undivided attention is a luxury in today's noisy world. Research shows that it takes only one to three minutes of us perusing through a magazine of too thin, too airbrushed, and too modified women, for us to close those slick pages and feel worse about ourselves.

Our celebrities of the eighties and nineties, Cindy Crawford, Linda Evangelista, and Christy Turlington, were all size 6's. By today's standards, they would be considered plus-sized models. Beauty was glamorized more than ever before in history, but twenty years ago, the average fashion model weighed 8% less than the average American woman. Today she weighs 23% percent less.

Although media is doing their fair share of brainwashing us into believing beauty looks a certain way, we are the ones who walk inside the stores and endorse the companies that make us (and our children) starve our way to their racks. Take *Abercrombie and Fitch's* controversial billboards, which have replaced those of *Calvin Klein* in our era. As our bodies are first awakening to feelings of sexual desire, advertisers are defining whom we should notice. They illustrate what's *sexy* and *cool* and what's not. Malnourished looking models draw the attention of adolescent children whose bodies are changing to become the women and men of today. The ads are especially effective because they target a critical point in their physical development; the time when the change in hormones and bodies will affect their adult self-concept.

On behalf of his brand, *Abercrombie* CEO Mike Jeffries remarked, "In every school there are the cool and popular kids, and then there are the not-so-cool kids—candidly, we go after the cool kids. We go after the attractive all-American kid with a great attitude and a lot of friends. Many people don't belong [in our clothes], and they can't belong. Are we exclusionary? Absolutely." Indeed the multibillion-dollar brand does not offer clothes above size 10. This marketing is weight discrimination. Companies who favor a business model of exclusion to impressionable tweens and adolescents are perpetuating prejudice and bullying.

As our culture begins to dramatize male attractiveness, anorexia in men and boys is rising at alarming rates. To complicate matters, despite nearly one-third of teenage boys using unhealthy weight control behaviors, such as skipping meals, fasting, smoking cigarettes, vomiting, and taking laxatives, the treatment options for men vs. women are far less available. Thankfully, we're becoming more conscientious. After creating a petition on Change.org that gathered more than 73,000 signatures, Benjamin O'Keefe caught the retailer's attention enough to meet face to face with Abercrombie to discuss ways to improve their harmful branding. Shortly after the meeting, an *Abercrombie & Fitch* spokesperson released the following statement:

"We look forward to continuing this dialogue and taking concrete steps to demonstrate our commitment to anti-bullying in addition to our ongoing support of diversity and inclusion. We want to reiterate that we sincerely regret and apologize for any offense caused by comments we have made in the past which are contrary to these values."

A week later, the company issued a college scholarship to students who had endured bullying. This compensatory action was a testimony to the power of our unified voices, votes, and dollars. Competing retailers heard the message loud and clear, and will think twice before following in the footsteps of A&F.

Victoria's Secret

Breasts are as American as apple pie. Women are constantly talking about one another's breasts. We're in an endless debate of whether breasts are too big or too small, to hide them or show them off. Push up bras, breast enhancement, breast reductions, and lifts are all popular investments. In the last fifteen years alone, the average bust size among North American women has increased from 34B to 36C.

Like it or not, physical attractiveness is an important element in women's psyche. With media being replete with images of full-breasted, thin women, Barbara Fredrickson, a professor of psychology at the University of North Carolina, explains the connection between the internalization of these images and social anxiety inside an objectification theory, in particular, the fear of public embarrassment and of not being good enough to measure up to a societal standard. Our culture encourages young girls and women to develop a view of themselves from an outside perspective. Social anxiety is becoming so much of a problem that even the military is willing to give generous, free breast enhancement procedures to service women who have severe stress and self-consciousness due to their *insufficient* proportions.

Days away from a birthday, that would drastically increase my risk of breast cancer (given family history), a cyst which had raised a brow at my last semi-annual visit had seemingly grown. Fear wrapped itself around my neck like a boa constrictor as they told me further exploration was necessary. Its grip continued slowly to tighten as each test necessitated the need for another. My loud extroversion became unrecognizably quiet and demure as I waited for results in the following weeks. If you've never had to undergo the experience of having your breasts flattened out like a pancake for a mammogram, let me paint a picture of what's ahead. You stand there half-naked, completely vulnerable, and told to place your right breast on a giant machine that compresses it like a Panini maker. While holding your breath, the front of the machine rotates to take a panoramic scan of the breast tissue. Then the left side endures the same ordeal. The whole procedure is undignified for both you and the woman administering the torture.

Radiologist Assistant: "I'm so sorry I have to do this, but I have to do it. I know this is worse than ＿＿＿ (insert awkward example here)"

These are all the examples I've heard throughout the years: "the dentist,"…"the gynecologist,"… "having a baby." (Side note: Okay, seriously, it's not that bad! But, I have heard it all)

Me: "It's okay. I'm grateful for the machine. It saves lives."

Hailey, the assistant, separated my breast tissue from the breastplate, headed towards the machine's screen and gasped, "Whew, wow."

My heart stopped. I took a breath. It began to beat again. There was a pause as she noticed that her reaction was a bit out of term. After what felt like eternity, Hailey noticed the look of terror in my eyes and she was forced to break the silence. After assuring me, she wasn't able to make any medical diagnosis, she said, "You've lost a ton of breast tissue since you were last here. It must be the kids. Did you breastfeed?"

Was she freaking kidding me?! That is what she gasped over?! I thought I had cancer! I felt relived for maybe three seconds, almost immediately after my survival seemed secured I regressed into two decades of self-hatred. Like a movie montage, life replayed itself. The movie's main character: Breasts.

I think back to the first pink birth control packet purchased not because I was sexually active, but because I thought my breasts would grow. Next, boob exercises, then naturally breast enhancing herbal pills—I was young and naive, what can I say? Then, before my augmentation, it was the boob-sucker. My first real grown up paycheck was cashed in to purchase a high-tech bra costing $1,200.00, which literally suctioned my two breasts as a vacuum into a plastic dome-like contraption, that came coupled with a minicomputer. The two astronaut-like vaults suspended my breasts in a pressurized state for 10 hours straight. For three months, I hardly slept. The heavy space bra made it so that the only way to sleep was to lay stiff as a board on my back. When the compression came loose, an alarm (beep-beep-beep) noted the disengagement and then (beep-beep-beep) re-pressurized. After an interminable night of interrupted sleep, I applied moisturizer to the tiny red rashes that encircled my chest. Admittedly, there were results, but they were minimal.

When Nick proposed, I was still unconvinced my body was

attractive enough to be loved for what it was. Months before our wedding day, I lay unconscious on a gurney that slowly rolled me into surgery (not because I had cancer but because I hated my breasts). I can distinctly remember assuaging my anxiety by picturing the *Angels Runway Show* that would play on network television that evening. I looked forward to getting refitted into a new Victoria Secret's cup size. Nick didn't think the surgery was necessary. I agreed, it wasn't necessary, but it seemed like an easy solution to my neurosis. He was constantly competing for the attention I gave my breasts, and consequently my body dysmorphia. This imagined ugliness or body dysmorphic disorder (BDD) had me revisit my self-consciousness several times a day aggrandizing my deviation from perfection to the point of obsession. What I saw is not what others saw.

Mirrors were my enemy. Nick could touch me only with the lights off. I even asked that he not compliment me or else my self-deprecating Ms. Bunny would appear, louder than any words of adoration Nick had. My breasts represented all I disliked in myself: they weren't pretty enough, not big enough, not worthy of love ever lasting. Despite Nick's affirmations, I was convinced he deserved more, someone better. I feared one day someone better looking would grab his attention and he'd leave me. A boob job was a contingency plan.

Plastic surgery is a health risk, let's not make light of that, but after the surgery, the self-hatred lifted a bit. Several studies show it is common for breast-enhancing and weight-reduction procedures to have a lasting positive effect on well-being and psychological inadequacies, but this effect comes only when combined with positive introspection. If you are considering the surgery, my advice isn't whether to do it or not. This decision is truly a personal one, but be clear with yourself as to *why* you're doing it and what it is you're trying to solve. Measure it against health risks and make the decision conscientiously. Plastic surgery does not come with a certificate of validation, it is an extreme act and requires much thought. To head to the surgeon every time we recognize a perceived flaw puts the health of our bodies and minds at risk.

A prolonged pattern of destructive thinking does not get solved by a quick fix; it simply doesn't work that way. Ask sincerely what the real reason for surgery is for you: To feel better as a person, to get past a mental road block, or is it because you want to look normal? Identify what normal is, especially when dealing with issues of self-hatred and body dysmorphia that would cause you not to truly see yourself.

Certainly there are other parts of the body that we are not 100 percent confident in, however, recognize that it's only a perception, an interpretation. Choose to redirect those destructive thought patterns to healthy habits such as exercise that can benefit both your mental state and your body. Unlike the inherited looks we are born with, it is empowering to control our diet, and mental attitude, and to see its benefits.

Our partners love our bodies not because they are perfect, but because they are ours. I have chosen to share my body with my husband, to have him share in my body's pleasure as he has allowed me to share in his. After fourteen years together, we are as much a part of one another as we are of ourselves. His body is a mere extension of my own. I would not change his feet, his ears, or his anything—they are bits of him who have created our children. When we alter our bodies, we are erasing parts of our histories. It took time, but now I understand that *we love who we love not because of perfection, but because every single strand of hair has a story.* This reason is why plastic surgery is hard to evaluate. How do we draw a distinction between the self we see and the self we are? My rule of thumb: It is hard to discredit those procedures which help us better connect to our authentic self when the health risks are marginal in comparison. Confidence has us experience ourselves more fully... However, if the reason we undergo a procedure is to erase shame, as if there is something wrong with us as a person, surgery or any aesthetic procedure will only be a temporary solution.

Think about how many contestants of the Miss America pageant would be in the competition if plastic surgery weren't allowed. The pressure to be thin, beautiful, and big-breasted is a national obsession—beauty queens or not. It's understandable that the contestants seem to look more fit than the average woman, however, the body mass index of Miss America winners have averaged 16.9 percent (adults with anorexia generally have a B.M.I. below 17.5) since the new millennia. Since there are age parameters in Miss America, why not impose weight parameters on what we as Americans sanction as a beauty competition?

Second Brain

Studies now show that we have a certain amount of willpower each day. Habits are the shortcuts our brains use to engage in the right or wrong things. When self-control is needed to tackle challenges, the need for prolonged mental strength becomes essential. Having a balanced nutritional diet is our fuel to attaining that energy and increasing our will power. Like physical exercise, mental strengthening requires preparation and practice. When our body chemistry is out of balance, anxiety levels go up and our attention goes to reactionary thoughts—our habits, be they good or bad.

Starvation mode requires our bodies to work much harder to keep it together. Emotions are set on the defensive when we compromise logical thinking. The overall depletion of nutrients, which help mood regulation, makes our experiences seem more dramatic or more black and white. With low energy levels, it is easy to speak unkindly and make unhealthy choices. The preset recording of the Reservoir Cats is automated and played on a loop as our ancestral wiring signals high alert.

Consider the following: When you've skipped breakfast and are sleep deprived, it's harder to choose a bowl of whole grains and quinoa over a freshly fried, warm donut and hot chocolate at work. It is easier to just bite into the donut and punish yourself with self-criticism later. Moreover, this cheat provides an excuse to give up healthy eating for the rest of the day. Instead, consider choosing self-compassion and making mindful, nutritious choices in the next few hours. Moving out of starvation mode moves us into mindful habits for long-term happiness.

According to Professor William Whitehead, Ph.D., almost all chemicals, which affect our brain's reality, are located in the digestive system and are therefore intimately correlated to our states of mind. For this reason, it is thought anti-depressants work at a gut level. Mental disorders, once thought of as mere chemical imbalances, are now being examined under the scope of systems biology, or the mind-brain-gut-and-heart connection. What we unattractively call our *gut,* neuroscientists' call the *second brain.* Our second brain contains over 100 million brain cells and uses 30 neurotransmitters. Two particularly important neurotransmitters are produced in this region: the happiness hormone serotonin and the pleasure hormone dopamine—are 95 percent and 50 percent respectively. These two agents are essential to the development of our identities, feelings of safety and love, and a sense of closeness with others through bonding, ecstasy, and reward.

"Different foods signal pleasure both through the substances they contain and the chemicals they cause the gut to release," says Gianrico Farrugia, director of the Enteric Neuroscience Program at the Mayo Clinic. Food affects our emotions and perceptions. Just as stress can upset the stomach, the stomach can affect the brain.

Selling Sexy

As Chasers take on more than we can chew, there isn't enough time to sit down to savor real authentic food, let alone eat a proper meal three times a day. Bypassing our kitchens into pantries full of meal replacements, on-the-go energy solutions, and make-believe food has made us a generation of both the *unhealthy skinny* and the *heavy malnourished.* Stuck in bodies that don't match who we are inside has us driving up profits for plastic surgery clinics, weight-loss centers, and pharmaceutical companies, while our overall wellness goes down.

We take the miracle of our bodies for granted. We want to look better and feel better without having to sacrifice our palate or challenge self-discipline. I saw this first hand, as patients would ask to throw away their drive-through paper bags and super-sized soda cups, before signing their name on a dotted line to have the lingering, and newly consumed fat lasered off their bodies – they also were made fully aware that these treatments were to be short-lived unless a healthy lifestyle was incorporated. Patients tried convincing themselves they could eat whatever they wanted, come in *fat* (as they would say), get a little cellulite reduction, fat melting, or body contouring, and come out *sexy*. That process was the real business—not the melting of fat, but the selling of *sexy*. If sexy was equivalent to empowerment, I instead offer a definition assembled from an amalgamation of research: *Empowerment is a sense of freedom within our self-awareness resulting from our ability to control our choices and actions over our own self-directed, self-defined goals.*

But here's the dilemma: Healthy food isn't sexy. When was the last time you saw a commercial of a beautiful and hot woman with an appropriate B.M.I. sensuously biting down on a piece of broccoli with her inviting sensuous red lips? Instead, we're sold processed food with ingredients designed to be addictive, easy to consume, and cheap—a deadly and dangerous combination.

Healthy food isn't cheap, but it's an investment in the future. Becoming more mindful of what we consume is not just about looking good; it's about gaining strength and vitality so our external selves reflect who we are inside. Food awareness is body awareness and ultimately self-awareness. What you choose to eat and how often you choose to feed your body has a significant effect on self-care. Eating a minimum of three times daily is at the cornerstone of our daily lives; it helps us sustain healthy states of mind. Pause and take notice of your habits. Calorie restriction diets have become more and more popular as studies find a low-calorie intake may prolong lifespan. Yet, it's imperative to make sure the calories we do eat are the right calories, rich in nutritional value.

Eating disorders are the number one killer of any other mental illness. While some of us are starving ourselves to the invisible size, others are eating the pain away. Fast-acting diets eat away at our self-respect, yo-yo dieting messes with our biochemistry and thinking. Each time we break a promise to maintain the weight we lost in a crash diet (that never gave us a fighting chance in the first place), the Reservoir Cats come out to shame us, reiterating how weak our will is, and how incapable we are of measuring up to a beauty standard.

Americans, specifically our youth, are in a desperate need of more public awareness programs focused on the long-term effects of sugar, high-fructose syrup, and superficial additives. In 1998, 46 states, the District of Columbia, and 5 U.S. territories joined in a unified voice and sued the four largest U.S. tobacco companies in order to recover tobacco-related healthcare costs. As a result, the companies settled out agreeing to change their marketing practices as well as pay a stipend to the states for the caring of patients with smoke-related illnesses. This action helped to fund *The Truth* campaigns that have been seen by millions in the web. The awareness and prevention campaigns empowered our youth to push a grass-roots effort to healthier life choices to the tipping point of a cultural mind shift. Smoking is now more synonymous with *cancer* than it is with *cool*.

Can you imagine if a similar movement took hold for healthy eating? That movement is the challenge celebrity-chef, Jamie Oliver, is taking on. Despite the significance of balanced nourishment, food education is still not a requirement in school curriculums. Cafeterias still offer prepackaged snacks and serve highly saturated fat food trays. In the same way, as it is inappropriate to have cigarettes filled vending machines at school, equally inappropriate is habituating students into unhealthy eating choices they carry on to adulthood. Obesity is an epidemic in this country. It is predicted the children of this generation will be the first to have shorter lifespans than their parents. Passionate in his efforts, Oliver heads the *Food Revolution*—educating schools and communities on what exactly is in our yummy, cheap, toxic diets.

What may seem expensive now could be mitigating larger, more painful experiences and expenses later. Illness reminds us of this simple truth as heart disease, diabetes, and cholesterol take an emotional toll. Food grown from the earth and nourished by the sun can be highly effective in helping our incredible organisms of our bodies, to heal themselves. Imagine how things would be different if we were more informed about the vitamins & nutrients that come from the hands of local farmers than we are of the drugs manufactured by chemical laboratories. Many of us can list off the promises of Xanax, Adderall, and Lipitor before we can list the benefits of super foods (with high anti-oxidants and vitamins). Food is the single most important fuel in our bodies because whatever we choose to put in our mouths has an immediate effect on how we feel in the short-term and our survival rate in the long-term. Simply said: What we eat affects the way that we think.

Getting off the Treadmill

The cultural bias that being overweight is an individual's problem has made fat-shaming boot camps and exercise programs more popular than ever before. This ideology has convinced us that having average-looking bodies is a weakness of will. Workouts named *Insanity* are advertised with pride. Fat shaming is marketed as motivational. Analyze this business model: a program designed to tear you down before building you back up. This is brainwashing! Using social pressure to do so makes it even more effective.

We interlace our yoga practices with our extreme fitness programs. All in the name of balanced health and wellness, right? Now consider the high incident of Rhabdo sweeping our nation's hospitals. Rhabdo is rare and used to be something only diagnosed in elite athletes and military trainees after extreme fatigue and depletion. Now what used to be rare is becoming bragging rights. Over-exercising can causing muscle fibers to breakdown and release a protein called Myoglobin into our system, which can harm our kidney cells. Once again it is easy to blame the fat-shaming gyms and videos for forcing us to push our limits, but we all know it's the Reservoir Cats that are truly to blame, the voices that say, "toughen up, hate the fat more than you hate the pain."

Self-deprecation doesn't guarantee better future choices. In fact, inner dialogue can transform every morsel of food into a personal barometer of self-love or self-hate. Your life experience is dictated by that which holds the attention of your mind. Single-minded emphasis on weight vs. a holistic approach conditions us to support unhealthy ideals. Dr. Neff, a pioneer in the science of self-compassion, explains "Self-compassion is not about relating to ourselves kindly, [but rather to get off the] treadmill and ridding ourselves of this constant need to feel better than others, just so we can feel better about ourselves. Here is where self-compassion comes in."

Dr. Neff breaks down compassion to three components:

1. **Self-kindness** = Treat ourselves as we would a friend

2. **Common Humanity** = Embrace how imperfections define our humanness. Seeking not what makes us different, but what we share in common with others.

3. **Mindfulness** = becoming aware of our emotions and self-criticism and change our dialogue to reflect kindness.

Practicing self-compassion is a humanitarian act. By seeking to find our sameness, we stop trying to decipher and compete against those we perceive as better than we are. Imperfection is human. We are perfectly imperfect human beings. Reducing our body parts to pretty or ugly dishonors our sacred bodies. We close ourselves to the true purpose our vehicle grants us, to develop life, experience sexual pleasure, and connect intellectually. What could be more important than sharing our long, healthy lives with our loved ones?

CHAPTER 9

Removing the Mask

"Just as we are born into male or female bodies and minds, our truths and meaning are distinct. To love like a woman, care like a woman, and simply be a woman, is an honor. Valuing who we are by how we love makes us warriors of truth and light."

-Solange Jazayeri

*L*ove's impasse is that we still believe *all is fair in love and war.* To be more valiant, we suit up to show up. Edited personas with cumbersome, silly defenses battle a war that is not worth fighting. We're Joan of Arcs, pretending we're someone we're not, protecting our soul from direct contact, to fight Knights in shiny armors who aren't themselves either. Heavy swords keep us three feet away. Close enough to shout, but too far to listen. We chase love away before it has a chance to serve our spirit. Yet, it is love whom we call the coward. The irony is we're all looking through guarded peepholes, for sincere vulnerability, to feel safe, unsheathed. Scared, we wait for someone else to speak up first, to call out the truce. Only then, do we take off the arresting steel armors and embrace.

It takes tremendous courage to love without caution. Not just falling in love romantically, but to love for its own sake, and to say, "I love you even if you don't love me back—even if you chose not to stay." Distrust is much easier. Distrust values the pain of yesterday justifying the restrictions we place on love today. We don't live inside romantic comedies with ensured happy endings; love is personal. We

---

want to be the one responsible for our lover's happiness... only to later demand they be responsible for ours. Lack of reciprocity can leave us questioning whether our love is grand enough, worthy enough, or special enough. In addition, we forget that it is the giving of love, which is most important. Imparting love is its own recompense.

Vulnerability and Intimacy

At the end of the day, we all just want a place we can come home to that feels safe for us to disarm our impractical garb. In the words of poet Robert Frost, "Home is the place where, when you have to go there, they have to take you in." Asking for support unmasks the Chasers' need to be self-sufficient. We are left having to redefine success in terms of values instead of self-reliance. The clank of our armor's headpiece hitting the floor, bears our vulnerability, and reminds us we must rely on trust.

People, not our personas, grow relationships. Perpetuating the idea that we can handle more than the average human being sustains the Ms. Superwoman image; we think we're protected behind the shield of human doings until the day we accept we are human beings, allowed to say, "Mercy, I relent." Interpreting dependency as a weakness does not give us more control. On the contrary, we make lizards into dragons when we take on more roles and responsibilities than we are capable of handling on our own. We become resentful when the dragon's fire humbles us to our knees in desperation. Yet we are the ones who feed the dragons, not others. Every time we acquiesce to unrealistic demands in exchange for admiration, we reaffirm a debilitating strength. Soon those around us begin to believe we are self-reliant and they in turn feel indispensable, unimportant. Dejected, they walk away. Some never return, and left behind, we feel abandoned.

Feeling Connected

Our bodies are not only our own—they belong to our lovers, to our children, to the soul inside us that wants to transcend beyond the roles we've chosen. After seven months of pelvic rest and long, long months of bed rest because of my high-risk pregnancy, Nick's advances should've felt flattering. Instead, it was hard to respond. My body no longer belonged to me, or our intimacy. After pregnancy, the after-birth complications, and a new reality—a toddler wrapped around my leg with a nursing infant in arms—made this new body feel tired and haggard. Another person on top of it, grabbing at it, felt suffocating.

The dance of intimacy had a new tempo that I was too tired to dance. Closeness was impossible when *I* was hidden and confused. Lingerie was replaced by maternity wear. Motherhood and romance felt contradictory. Recovering from the backlash of babies taking over my body (like little aliens sucking the youth out of it) coupled with a husband that didn't let lactating breasts discourage his *needs*, made me lose ownership of my body altogether.

The two most important phrases our children need to hear are, *I love you, and I am proud of you.* They're also the two most important phrases we need to hear from our partners. We all need to be reminded that we're loved because of who we are, not because of the ease or proficiency with which we navigate challenges. When we first meet, we do our best to show flawlessness, masking our ugly parts to be perceived as attractive as possible. Nevertheless, by day's end, the makeup fades away to reveal our imperfections. Eventually we're seen as we are, bare-faced and naked. With the blemishes of our inner person exposed, in the most genuine and vulnerable of ways we face our lovers, and hesitantly ask, "Do you still love me like this?"

After weeks of excuses, the breakdown came: "I'm mourning myself. I love our babies but I'm lost, afraid, and feel guilty all the time. I am overwhelmed and sex is the last thing on my mind." Our lives are a series of coming together and instances of pulling apart. Only after saying these words aloud, between flowing tears, did the intimacy between Nick and I return. It was a plea for safety. I needed to know I was not alone in this. There was a need to feel that he, too, at least at some level, felt opposing, conflicting, ugly feelings.

Our partners are the sounding boards to us, determining whether we're doing a good enough job or acting in an appropriate manner. Maintaining his approval and pride was so important that admitting frustrations and inadequacies felt risky. The fear was that pointing out my inadequacies would draw attention to something he'd not perhaps seen. Once exposed, there would be no going back and hiding again.

Having met in college, Nick and I essentially grew up together, from students to professionals to parents. Each accomplishment and dream made possible drew us closer in our admiration for one another. Becoming parents is the single most unifying act two human beings can share, creating one being from the union of two. I didn't want his love or his pride for me to alter, although everything had changed. We had changed—we had evolved. He was the ultimate observer and critic. The love we shared, and what we created thus far, proved I was lovable – it was hard to be vulnerable for the sake of his validation. A negative opinion would have felt too grand and penetrating. However, the self I had been mourning, Nick assured me, was still there. While evolving, she had not been left behind.

Embracing Our Differences

We've survived among the species because of how well men and women fit together, like the pairing of our genders, our right and left hemispheres, counter-balance the logical with the emotional to become more astute. Evolutionary psychologists explain that women's psychological adaptations and evolutionary instincts are what have enabled our deep-rooted connection between our partners and offspring. We depend on our partners to help us realize we are strong enough, resilient enough, and worthy enough to continue our journey onward. Pleasure centers of the brain responsible for pairing and bonding activate when we make love. Researchers at the University of College in London studied the pleasure and reward centers of our brain to measure how oxytocin and dopamine affect our critical thinking when we are behaving affectionately. They found that a simple snuggle can activate oxytocin, which acts as a hormonal building block for trust. In another interesting study, the brains of new mothers were scanned while they observed pictures of their infant children. Then they compared their brain activity when photographs of their romantic partners were shown. The same love regions of the brain lit up for both. There is something very real about women falling in love with their sons and daughters, and men feeling the new competitor inside their arena.

Although both genders have the same amount of brain cells, how we use those cells is dramatically different. While men have secured safety physically, we have secured families emotionally. Women have relational and social advantage, while men have a systematic advantage. Given our preemptive and relational thinking, women's fear and anxiety response can quickly be activated into imagining today's unpaid bills as tomorrow's bankruptcy. Men are more linear thinkers. They concentrate on the problem at hand, a temporary bump in the road they need to solve today.

This long-term view and short-term focus is interdependence at its best—it is what kept our forebearers alive. Relationships have been central to securing our livelihood throughout time. Moving out of harm's way to safer ground is harder to do with children strapped to our bodies and toddlers in tow. This is why the anticipated fear is higher in women than it is in men. Therefore, the need for security and shelter is instinctual to our genetic makeup.

By modern standards, our survival and that of our family remains higher when there is long-term pairing. In the Framingham Offspring Study (that tested 3,682 adults over a ten-year span), the benefits of marriage for men were clear, even after taking out the major contributors of risk. With cardiovascular-related health problems, married men had a forty-six percent lower mortality rate than unmarried men.

We may not need to rely on men, but we do need men and men need us! Saying aloud, "I want to fall in love and get married instead of building a lifelong career" shouldn't be embarrassing. Certainly, we don't all want an institutional commitment, but every woman does need supportive intimate relationships. Even virgin nuns describe being in love with their G-d and working daily at experiencing more closeness in their relationship with Him.

Independence has been confused with the denouncing of men. Nevertheless, despite our want for separation, our love for men keeps drawing us back to them. There's an inner need in each of us for love. The fear Chasers have of being seen, as too co-dependent is so great, we now mistake co-dependent relationships to mean any relationship where our happiness and well-being *includes* another person.

"I just don't want to be needy, but...". Needy has become a catch phrase to minimize our needs for secure attachments. Society has convinced us that our happiness should be attained in isolation; this only leads to aloneness, depression, and stress. The next time the judgmental voice of your inner Rosie says, "I can do it by myself. I don't need a man," remember that having needs doesn't make us the weaker sex nor does needing protection and security show a lack of independence, it only proves we're human.

When we feel connected, secure, and loved, we come alive. Dependency is not a bad thing, but a necessary biological need. In fact, dependency is what breeds independence and interdependence. When we can rely on our partners to be supportive and encouraging, we're better able to tap into our inner resilience and grit. Their encouragement as our cheerleaders lifts the heaviness of guilt, insecurity, and fear that arrest us so we may take on steeper climbs.

Healthy Dependence

Co-dependent and needy are mainstream and interchangeable terms, when in fact, the term co-dependency, was originally formulated to describe a particular relationship between those who suffer alongside their addictions and/or alcoholic partners. Co-dependence is an imbalanced relationship where a healthy reciprocation does not exist (i.e. one person is feeding off the other in a synergetic way). To review: it's not co-dependent to need our father's emotional support, or male friendships for perspective, or to need a man to make love to. Admittedly, some of us don't need men to do the latter. We may not need to marry men or be financially supported, but we need them nonetheless and let's not be convinced out of it. Not just men, but we need good men: strong uncles, nurses, managers, presidents, etc. In today's economy more than ever before, men and women both want partners who will give us emotional, financial, and spiritual support.

Committed partnerships evolve people. In the sharing of information, as we pair up, categories of knowledge are divided, allowing each helpmate a degree of expertise. This aiding in problem solving and calibration of our natural tendencies strengthens our knowing of self. I am not suggesting women should not be self-sufficient. On the contrary, I am saying all meaningful professions from parenting to medicine need both genders involved. In us all lives a feminine and masculine duality— finding our own balance of the two is what makes us a unique family. We may be able to do what men can do (and vice versa), however, we're our best inside our implicit natures, learning from one another, cooperating and not competing or assimilating.

The human race has a life insurance plan: children. Our choosing of a resourceful man is as natural as men desiring a healthy (yes, symmetrically attractive) woman—it is evolution's way of ensuring strength and adaptability. Our courtship with men is more scientific than we often realize. An openly affectionate and approachable woman is a good investment of time and focus for a man. They can afford to divert their attention to a place where their pay-off would be their genes living onto the next generation.

Women too need to know they have a responsible, resourceful man who will be patient, and supportive if the necessity arises in the future (in case his seed fertilizes). Unfortunately, the pill has watered down this courtship. In dissociating our pregnancy risk from our sexual encounters, we have replaced our emotional needs for our carnal ones.

Women want dependable men and men want women who need them. Taking on the role of men is not working. Feminizing men to be more like us is not working either. Men have, and always will have, an important role to play in women's lives. The idea is for us to evolve together, to allow men to be more emotional and women to be more assertive – in ways that are natural to both genders. Men have a different way of communicating, but they too, want more freedom to express themselves without being viewed as feminine.

We say we want strong, emotionally available communicative men, but when we sense fear or vulnerability in them, the truth is, it scares us. Our instincts go on red alert because they're supposed to protect us. It's an instinct—but we're evolving out of that, and we're becoming more responsible for one another. Here's a scary statistic: men are four times more likely to die of suicide than women are. Surely, the fact that men don't have the same emotional freedom or emotional support as we do is one of the factors. Women's friendships are many, some intimate, some long lasting, some friendly but transitory. Men, on the other hand, are much more selective, often because trust in their minds must be earned.

Learning more about our gender differences and honoring those differences, helps us interconnect. Men for example, find intimacy by communicating side by side through physical activity. The face-to-face interaction is women's way of communicating as we are engineered to read facial expressions. Men spent hours, even days, in the wild talking to their hunting tribesmen while on guard, vigilant for potential threat. Face-to-face communication of hot topics can feel attacking and intrusive for them. Men bond physically. This is why we watch them roughhouse our children and toss our babies up in mid-air as we cringe. Nevertheless, when we demand men communicate like women, we ask them to change who they are and to be more like our girlfriends, and in that subtlety we stop listening to different ways in which communication expresses itself.

Evolving Together

From the most intimate and sacred of unions, two individuals merge as co-Creators to Life. Looking at the mosaics of our combined ancestry, our children make the existential real. These little untethered spirits placed in our arms, and laid on our chests, expand the depths of our hearts and the meaning of our lives. To protect our defenseless kin, the independent man and the interdependent woman stop flirting and build a home together.

Mothers don't have a monopoly on parenthood. Fathers make sons and daughters more independent and more aware of their physical strength and aptitude. According to research conducted by Nielsen Media, the influence of fathers on the lives of their daughters can generally have a stronger impact than that of their mothers. Well-fathered daughters have a greater ability to trust and interact with men in their adult relationships. They're usually more self-confident, self-reliant, and perform better scholastically and in their careers than do poorly fathered daughters.

Man's energy was made to complement ours. The relationships our children grow up observing in us as parents, and in the leaders who surround them, will set the stage for how they will communicate, cooperate, and solve problems when they reach adulthood. Bringing a masculine presence into the lives of developing young minds is essential for them to embrace their feminine and masculine duality. According to the Center for Disease Control, 85% of all children who show behavior disorders come from fatherless homes – 20 times the average.

Just as our mothers and grandmothers were professional pioneers, so too are men of this millennia pioneers in the domestic lifestyle. We're coming back to the cooperative relationships of the hunter-gatherer days. Women hunted and gathered too, differently when they were pregnant of course, but they were just as respected as men were and men helped women raise their young. Women are now being asked to support men in this transition. The commercials that used to mock men's inability to do the laundry are being replaced by detergent ads targeting stay-at-home fathers. The *Ultimate Test* Huggies, announced last year:

"To prove Huggies diapers and wipes can handle anything, we put them to the toughest test imaginable. We left Dads alone with their babies, in one house, for five days, while we gave moms some well-deserved time off. How did Huggies products hold up to daddyhood?"

Presumably, women are better equipped at changing diapers... Imagine if there were a commercial promoting a new medical technology where female physicians were the *Ultimate Test,* in which the machinery would have to be *good enough* to withstand. Huggies has since apologized and changed their messaging. Let's be thankful—maybe with men's pull in media, the much-deserved respect domestic life has needed will finally rise.

Out of the Darkness

We're the surviving ambitious women of the new Millennium, a metamorphic adaption of our ancestors' lineage surviving throughout the ages. Out of the darkness of the caves and the enlightenment of the Renaissance, our insatiable drive to do more, be more, and achieve more has made us seek out new challenges and cross new frontiers.

Motherhood makes our past identities sacrificial lambs that we humbly relinquish for love; offering up our independence, our bodies, all we knew ourselves to be, and in doing so we are brought to our knees in love, joy, despair, and hope. Raising children often redefines us, changing the focus from achievement to legacy building. We come to recognize that praise is not what ultimately fulfills us, but the reaching inward for courage and resilience, and the reaching out to those we love that brings us inner peace. It was only after I was honest about what I needed for myself that our family life, our intimacy, our connection together began to change.

CHAPTER 10

Trust and the Tribe

"Of one thing you can be certain: every person you see—no matter the race, religion, political beliefs, body type, or appearance—is family."
Dieter F. Uchtdorf (Religious Leader of the Church of Jesus Christ)

*W*e're all part of the same human race. Sometimes we forget that. We divide into camps, but the truth remains that we all affect each other, each day, in every way. As cliché as it sounds, sometimes we have to look back and recognize what we already know intuitively to move forward.

Before there were parcels of land with fences to divide us, marriages and trade were the alliances that built the social contract. Clans pooled together the resources of neighboring tribes, and although love was the spirit of the tribe, it was trust and faith which held it together. Human beings are meant to live in community; we're not meant to survive on our own. Our evolution comes from exchanging ideas with one another so we may grow in our collective wisdom. It's easy to blame our neighbor, our enemies, other nations, or anyone else for the injustices of the world when in fact, each of us are responsible. Not because of us individually, but because we have not truly joined in relative harmony. It's not only what we do, but also what we allow others to do that matters. Collective wisdom and strength are the **real** powers of the tribe.

The Sum of its Parts

Breaking bread and looking one another in the eye has remained an emblematic symbol of trust throughout the ages. Men and women shared their provisions for the sake of togetherness. It is a gift to belong to a table where elders impart wisdom, adults give guidance, and the young remind us all of humanity's most important and basic of principles: treat others with the same respect that you deserve. But as our tribes of origin live further and further apart and children's perception of the tribe gets replaced by soccer teams, rotating single parent homes, and endless homework, breaking bread has become harder and harder.

It takes a village to raise consciousness. Think of New York as a microcosm of the world. The people of Little Italy, the immigrants in Chinatown, and Brooklyn's Orthodox Jews all living side-by-side, yet in their own distinct communities. The occupations adults undertake enhance the expertise of the group. Neighbors help neighbors and mothers help mothers. In this way, each individual enriches New York's culture. Interestingly enough, food happens to finds its place at the center of it all. Religious or not, to be reminded of our rich history is a practice we all could bring to our dinner tables. Sitting amongst families in such types of feasts where the food is blessed with gratefulness, the candles lit in reverence, and where our ancestors' lineage are all acknowledged and praised, can bring great perspective. Familial and cultural rituals take a stronger role in weekly counsel than any influence government politicians could ever provide. Even if our families are scattered and we don't attend Sunday mass, if we opt to nurture friendships, the doctrine of unity is likely to make its way to neighborhood grill-outs.

The point is different colored shirts of rivaling sports teams can't stop ceremonial barbecues where the clanking of beer bottles and the flailing arms become the true background noises to our storytelling and advice giving. Much more than food is being dispensed at family gatherings. Who better than family to *tell it like it is*? Those who are closest to us understand what painful triggers may cause us shame or distrust and instead of judging us, they can bring to light our reactive or defensive behavior.

We sometimes forget how important it is to touch base and truly engage with one another before we run out the door with a hot pocket in hand (so we can engage with others who are not as close and don't necessarily have our best interest in mind). In The National Longitudinal Survey of Adolescent Health, Musick and Meier found evidence to support that having regular family meals together while growing up increases the likelihood of life-long healthy eating habits, decreases our chances of addictions, and increases our overall positive outlook.

The stories of our relatives become embedded in our memories and so do the lessons they have learned and passed onto us – like the nuances of knowing who else in our family shares our musical talent. We forget how valuable our individual happiness is to those who came before us and those who will come after. The history of sacrifice of our motherland can be lost when we take for granted the sacrifices our ancestors made to bring forth a better life for us. No matter what our past is, we are here because our lineage has persevered, and in this way, we can too.

Accepting the Truth

Feeling proud of only one side of our family history, casts a shadow on the other half of our family identity. When we hide parts of our lineage, we begin to believe that at some level we come from a place that must be hidden, forgotten, and denounced. Most of us have a list of *castaways* in our family lines, but individualism lessens our sense of togetherness. Ill deeds are a personification of pain. Rarely, if ever, is there malicious behavior without a history of sickness or ignorance behind it—often passed down from a previous generation.

It is easy to judge and find faults, but learning to find kindness inside ourselves for those closest (yet most psychologically distant) has us practice our compassion, stretching our humanity where it hurts the most, while also developing our spiritual growth. Kindness in some form can be found if we choose to let down our guard and view the full spectrum of a human being.

Individualism has fueled us into taking the preemptive strike of isolating ourselves. Standing apart from one another, we focus on what benefits *me and mine* not *us and ours*. When any member of the family is cast out and *forgotten,* we all lose. Not everyone can be invited to the dinner table. There are those who don't know how to mind their manners and speak out of turn, or are greedy and haven't yet learned respect. Nonetheless, leave the door open for one day they may be the honored guest who imparts the lessons from learned wisdom.

She Said, He Said

Romantic quarrels shouldn't supersede the protection of a family's advancement. Two lovers who've zeroed in on their physical attraction for one another can be blinded to the struggles of long-term commitments. A commitment to our communion, by accepting counsel, can be help to maintain the strength of a family over time. When a religion is not there to guide us, the power of a group (the idea that two minds are greater than one) may be what it takes us to accept that there is a power greater than we are. The true catastrophe of divorce is that children aren't the only ones asked to pick a side in a separation. The breakdown of a partnership underscores all the elements of the extended family structure, which built our appreciation for community, rituals, gatherings, and the transitive trust and loyalty between one another. All of these things can be jeopardized with an unhealthy separation.

Uncompassionate alliances are formed to prove loyalty in divided camps. We ask our friends and family to rally around us in anger and pain so we may feel accompaniment when the partnership is dismantled and we are left feeling vulnerable and alone. Petty quarrels then arise and judgment cuts the braided cord of family ties. Left behind are two untied lineages standing vulnerable to their own unraveling. Dysfunctional marriages may be painful and hard, but so are the *remember whens* and the *look how far we have come* memories that get lost in the shuffle. Commitment isn't staying in a marriage that doesn't work; it is staying committed to working it out. We can leave our marriages psychologically without signing the papers physically. That requires both partners to work together at forming a better partnership, be it inside or outside a marriage. Many times, we can be guided back to one another, at least as friends. This act is the Discipline of Love. This discipline is practiced not only for the sake of children, but also for the sake of our own personal evolution. Working at becoming a better parent may not make us better partners, but working at becoming better partners will make us better friends and parents.

We Belong Together

Stress is a humanitarian response. It's our biology acknowledging we're part of a tribe. After a decade of studying the negative effects of stress, Stanford University psychologist Kelly McGonigal is now studying its positive effects. She recently gave a commanding speech in the Ted Talks platform strongly stating, "Stress makes us socially smart." She explains that our bodies are alerted to stress by neurochemicals released from our heart, one of which is oxytocin. Oxytocin, remember, is known as the cuddle hormone because our body releases it when we give and receive affection. However, this cuddle hormone, as she points out, also is a stress agent that makes us crave social interaction. As McGonigal puts it, "It's a built-in mechanism for stress-resilience." As we offer and accept help from others, we're better able to recover from the negative effects of stress.

We cannot avoid stress in our lives, but we can be better at handling it and transforming it into something constructive. To prove her point, 1,000 Americans ages 34 to 93 were studied. Two questions were asked of them: 1) How much stress have you experienced in the last year, and 2) How much time have you spent helping friends, neighbors, and people in your community?

Five years later, they tracked down those who participated. For every major, stressful experience, mortality rate increased by 30 percent, **except** in those individuals who found the time to help others. For those tribes-men and women, there was no negative stressful impact on their death rate. By allowing stress to motivate our connection to others, we affirm to ourselves, as Dr. McGonigal notes, "...I can trust myself to handle life's challenges, and remember that I don't have to face them alone." The tribe mentality mitigates the stress of everyday life. Our coming together in harmony reminds us of who we are inside the collective. In *giving* we learn to *accept*. Collaboration restores trust, as it is an act of faith.

Rebuilding Trust

Faith pursues transformation; converting anxiety into peace, rancor into compassion, fear into acceptance, and it is love that makes that transformation possible. The dilemma of Chasers is that the fragmentation of the American family has weakened our trust in humanity. Our need for independence has sunk us in the quicksand of trying to *do it all* and *be it all*, and our energies are exhausted as we try to clamor our way out alone.

No one escapes the feelings of vulnerability and desperation. Exchanging a degree of privacy for counsel makes family and friends the lifeline to our regaining strength. Close relationships are our primary source of happiness because we are appraised for who we are across all dimensions and scenarios, not who we are in just one snippet of our lives, but who we have proven to be across time. Childhood friendships and siblings are powerful in this way because our self-concept and histories formed together. We are able to take into consideration the traumas that formed our inadequacies and personalities. Accepting the advice builds emotional learning. As we open ourselves to be analyzed, we practice the art of listening without defensiveness. We do not need a multitude of friends or close family, but studies do show we need at least one confidant we can trust, someone able to step into our shoes and understand the intentions behind our behavior, someone who can *anticipate* and provide help when we need it.

Divide and Conquer

Keeping the tribes at work and at home happy is hard and adding your children's school tribe to the mix is a formidable task. We try our best to do what we can and when we can't we are forced to delegate. Let's be honest here—delegation isn't always done in respectful ways. Childless women are often asked to step in when parents feel the pull of their personal lives dragging them away from work, stay-at-home mothers often volunteer to help in the imbalance of working parents, and those children who don't have parents often rely on the community to feed, clothe, and raise them. It doesn't always feel fair when we take on responsibilities that are not our own, but when we do so, we could shift our mind to an intrinsic sense of altruism, a practice from our own humanity. We don't always get to see how our giving helps us first hand, but isn't feeling part of something greater a reward itself?

Part of our discomfort stems from us not fully accepting we are all part of the same community. When we work together, we thrive together, but first we must respect our individual choices.

Women Warriors

My first experience inside the shooting range of working vs. stay-at-home moms came in the first days of Isadora's very first school year. Eight mothers walked into a room full of colorful pictures, hanging fish, and knee-high seating for a school volunteer committee. It must have been funny to witness grown women trying to have a serious meeting, sitting with our knees poking at our faces in an aqua room with design elements that appeal to 5-year-olds. I have to say, initially, I was thrilled to be part of the group. Feeling completely detached to my kid-free friends and my business colleagues, I was excited to start a new family-friendly group. Being an extrovert by nature, I missed my social life. My old friends couldn't relate to dirty diapers, tantrums, and ballet schedules. The loneliness was messing with my head so bad that I began to wonder who my friends would be if I lived on *Sesame Street*. **This** would be my first attempt at making mom friends, and I thought volunteering would be a perfect way to help the school and set up some playdates.

The morning of the meeting, I carefully selected my outfit—not too short, tight, or flashy, and most definitely minimal makeup. Giving myself a little pep talk, "If I can make it in business, I can make it in kindergarten," I sat next to a mom who wobbled over with a bright pink neon cast on her left leg. She seemed nice, a little loud, but funny nonetheless. The perfect playdate candidate I thought... until the loud and funny turned into obnoxious and irritating. The minute we started to divide the work, her brows furrowed and her upper lip tightened as she lashed out at the group and said, "It isn't fair that the teachers and the volunteers end up doing all the work." She was quite upset always to find herself amongst the *usual suspects*, assembling ornaments for Christmas, cutting paper antlers at Thanksgiving, and recruiting volunteers for fundraisers.

I was no longer glad I'd made it to this meeting. This mother's negative tone brought out the fighter in me. Almost instantly my defenses went up, and my body got tense. I expected to find nice, kind ladies at the volunteer group, gathering to make school crafts over glasses of Chardonnay. I know the wine was unrealistic, but I was hoping for it anyway – and as it turned out, it certainly would have helped make the experience much more pleasant. I sat next to my biggest fear: the ultra-conservative, hypercritical super mom. Being surrounded by childhood images like the Little Mermaid reservoir in the room suddenly rekindled my own kindergarten memories. I imagined myself out-shouting her, but my daughter's teacher was there and I still had my eye on other moms as potential playdates.

The work was, no doubt, annoying. It required taking little intricate pieces of paper and cutting around the edges to fit them perfectly together like a jigsaw puzzle. I didn't understand how this mother was so angry at being there when no one had forced her to volunteer. She went on to explain that last year she had done the bulk of the crafting work that other professional career moms had apparently slacked on. To be honest, she didn't really label them working moms, she simply alluded to lazy parents in general. I made the auto-correction in my head, concluding that one day I might be typecast as a lazy, career mother. In her defense, she appealed for sympathy by saying, "I know we are all busy. I have small twins at home and my schedule is crazy too, but I **still** find the time to be there for my children." She rounded off that sarcastic comment with, "I guess some of us care more than others."

Her identity rested upon how much she was able to do for her children and how many hours she punched in to the volunteer time card. The room stood quiet but frazzled, like walking into a country western saloon after a gunfight. She looked at us all with a smirk on her face as if to say, "I know that is what you are all thinking, don't you agree?" Only, I didn't agree and by the silence (and the look in the other mothers' faces), it seemed like they didn't agree either. Yes, we're all busy, but no, we don't really want to be doing kindergarten cutouts for fun and we're all here for the same reason. We all want the best for our children and we all want to contribute. Although I was there that day, it was likely that one day in the future I'd be too busy to volunteer and would need other moms to help me. When you're a team player, your team won't let you fail. When you drop the ball, there's always someone to pick it up. I thought we were all part of the mom team now.

So I broke the silence by saying, "I understand your frustration, but I don't think the issue is that parents don't care or that other things are more important. I think life sometimes catches up to us all, and we're left doing the best we can with the situation. I have time right now, so I can take on a bigger load. Maybe we can ask those parents who don't have time to chip in some money and we can hire someone to help to make up for their parts." After I finished, the room broke out in laughter. I felt like I'd been left out of the joke. It wasn't mean spirited, but they still were laughing at my expense.

After the laughing quieted, a woman injected, "Every parent would just pay, Solange. No one has the time. Wouldn't you pay if you had the option?"

"Good point," I conceded. They were right. We're all trying to barter for more time one way or another. There was no negotiating at this table. The moms were not ready to rally behind this angry lady, but no one was going to side with my Polly Anna attitude either. When the terminator mom eyes next to me pointed in my direction with glaring disapproval, I repeated, "We're all just doing the best we can."

Another mother chimed in, "Yes, we are, I needed the help last year so I am happy to give it this year."

On my way to the parking lot, one of the mothers approached me and asked if I was okay. "I was a little concerned for you there," she said. "It looked like she was going to bite your head off. I think she may have been drunk."

I appreciated this gesture tremendously because I initially walked away from the meeting feeling as if my playdate calendar would be as vacant as my high school Friday nights. "I never realized mommy wars were that blatant. If I had baby twins running around causing havoc in addition to a busted up leg, maybe I would be drinking too before walking into mommy central," I replied.

We are all part of the same tribe. We all need help in one way or another. If volunteering at a school helps another woman get a promotion so she can show my daughters what is possible for a woman in the workplace, I believe the extra effort is worth it. The point is this: for each one of us to rustle up to our full potential so that the tribe itself can prosper, we need to make sacrifices, concession, and aid one another. It's a symbiotic system that may not always pay with the same currency (be it time or money). Mothers of all types allow for our sons and daughters to see the potential of their unlimited choices. The women we volunteer our hours for today may be mentoring our children tomorrow.

I have two daughters who are incredibly different in character much like the difference I see between my own two sisters. Different lifestyle choices fit different personalities. Our contribution to our community comes in many forms. The contribution of stay-at-home mothers, career mothers, and childless women, help our community thrive in its diversity.

The Final Frontier

The final frontier is not loving our neighbor, but loving our enemy and seeing ourselves in them. Having an unconditional respect for the inner being that exists in us all—beyond the imperfections of personalities—unites us in to the universal worthiness of the human spirit. It is an essential step towards the pursuit of unconditional love. Humanists explain the atrocities of the world as ignorance or mental affliction and pursue knowledge and wisdom to understand malice better. It is much easier to be kind to the ignorant and sick than it is for us to be kind to someone we typecast as malevolent.

Peacekeepers like Mother Theresa do not see a celestial hierarchy. "Let us not use bombs and guns to overcome the world. Let us use love and compassion. Peace begins with a smile. Smile five times a day at someone you don't really want to smile at. Do it for peace." Her energy was directed to growing compassion not competition. Love, too, is a growth process that must be exercised so it may grow in strength. Mother Theresa would not participate in rallies that fought and protested wars—having a clear understanding of her core principles— she stood only for peace. She believed in cooperation; helping a Hindu become a better Hindu, a Muslim a better Muslim, and a Catholic a better Catholic. Separateness is our human limitation. *Oneness* is loving one another just as the act of loving oneself. Unconditional love has faith in the intrinsic worthiness of the present self without requirements for the future or dependence on the acts of the past.

Stepping Out in Faith

When women began to have the choice to have a life apart from what traditions dictated, our entire lives fell under scrutiny. Religion and birth control were at odds, so we swallowed the pill as if to say, "I choose me over a religion that only allows for Him, a man, to make decisions." We lost faith that a Higher Power had us—the feminine *she*—in mind because we only heard the words *he* and *him*.

Believing that life rested on our hands, that the choices we made to delay motherhood bought us the dream, led us to the ultimate delusion—that we truly are the givers of life. Moreover, this delusion had us aggrandize our power at the cost of our faith.

To some degree, we had to reconcile the new power we held. In addition, when the life we've crafted doesn't fair us well, we blame that other Higher Power. Yet, when we find success, we claim it as our luck, hard work, and dedication. Choices made exclusively for our betterment, had us turn our backs on what, in reality, may slow down our G-d-given right to progress our inner spiritual growth. We know deep within there's more out there, we experience emptiness at a cellular level when we credit ourselves entirely, and focus on external rewards, rather than our humanity.

Distrusting that a Higher Power leads us, we have turned to money, status, and perceived independence. Today we pay the price...

By believing we had to overcome and find retribution for what has been done to women, we failed to acknowledge this is a step in our identity evolving– if we choose to come together, we may, in fact, find a common voice, and bring more compassion to the world.

According to the Dalai Lama, *[Biologically],females have more sensitivity towards others' pain or suffering. Scientists also [are] saying that. Now, in the 21st century, is the time we really need more effort for promotion of human compassion. In that respect, females have a more important role."*

CHAPTER 11

Chasing the Illusion

"I see in the fight club the strongest and smartest men who've ever lived. I see all this potential and I see squandering. God damn it, an entire generation pumping gas, waiting tables, slaves with white collars, advertising has us chasing cars and clothes, working jobs we hate so we can buy shit we don't need. We're the middle children of the history man, no purpose, or place, we have no Great war, no Great depression, our great war is a spiritual war, our great depression is our lives. We've been all raised by television to believe that one day we'd all be millionaires and movie gods and rock stars, but we won't and we're slowly learning that fact... and we're very, very pissed off."

- Chuck Palahniuk, *Fight Club*

𝓕rom the minute we're born, we begin to die, and from this great urgency, we search for meaning. So many of our choices, we believe, have been made for us. Perhaps to some degree they have. The lives we're born into are, after all, a product of someone else's. Fifty percent of happiness is genetic, ten percent stems from environmental factors, and then there's that remaining forty percent... Here, in this gap, between what's ours and what remains to be created, our choices illuminate our consciousness. This forty percent gap is the sweet spot, where the *Why*, and the meaning of all things exist, where *we* decide who and what to worship. Why is it, then, that we continue to chase other people's dreams? Chase tomorrow at the cost of today? Moreover, why, why, why after all we have been given, do we continue to fight the good fight—with ourselves? **What will it take us to choose a higher consciousness, so we may elevate the deeper meaning of our lives?**

The End of the Rainbow

Culturally, we're not only inclined, but also taught to ask for more of what's measurable, rather than cultivating real meaning for what we have at our disposal. Experts often talk about a certain kind of emptiness (a very real phenomenon in human neuropsychology) resulting from societal structures which teach us only to be good workers, and good consumers—not happy and fulfilled human beings. The presumption that we're entitled to prosperity without commitment or authenticity has left us hollow. Not only that, appropriating success to our own independent doing makes our lives a scorecard of checks and balances – which has, in turn, depleted our emotional bank accounts, leaving us relatively unhappy as we search for the next thing.

Professor Sonja Lyubomirsky of the University of California, Riverside suggests that altruism may be the key to raising our happiness baselines. She's spent years researching and analyzing the how-to's to well-being—how to raise it and how to sustain it. Altruism, she and her colleagues have found, is an important component to raising our happiness *set points*. Funding our emotional bank accounts and constructing new realities can elevate our consciousness—we can learn to practice authenticity by intentionally habituating who we are, to how we live. However, to do this we have to be brave enough to let go of society's deepest held misperceptions (and misrepresentations). Take for example the notion that money buys us more choices and, therefore, more happiness. A study by University of British Columbia and Harvard Business School asked 429 people (with incomes ranging from $5,000 to over $200,000) to rate their happiness. Next, they asked participants to rate what they perceived their own happiness and the happiness of others would be at higher or lower earnings. The results: an estimation of how much happiness money can buy.

Earnings	Predicted happiness	Actual happiness	
$10,000	13.25	50	= 3x higher than predicted
$25,000	23.39	70	
$35,000	33.73	72.55	
$55,000	49.44	76.29	= lower than predicted
$90,000	66.10	74.53	
$125,000	73.28	67.05	
$160,000	76.04	79.54	
$500,000	77.27	78.56	

According to Professor Dunn and lead author Lara Aknin, the preconceived notions we have are incongruent with what money affords us when accounting for the added commitments we often shoulder at higher salaries. As we get on our hedonic treadmill, more luxury is desired to satisfy basic needs, and so we buy shinier, bigger, better things. These expenditures add up. The stress of floating the mortgages, car payments, and a more expensive lifestyle make us prisoners. In addition, the fear that we may lose it all, if the money faucet runs dry, can strain our overall well-being. "[People] forget that those with lower incomes might actually be working less or doing jobs that don't pay as well, but are deeply satisfying or are less stressful," said Dunn. The study showed the biggest discrepancy in predicted happiness and actual happiness between the $10,000 income level, where happiness was three times higher than predicted, and $55,000 salary group, where happiness was actually lower than forecasted. Those participants at the $90,000 range and above had happiness levels that were relatively constant.

Although it's true that money funds more choices, it also can compound anxiety. When choices are limited, we know exactly what we need to do to be satisfied. A plethora of choices, on the other hand, has us constantly weighing what's *better* as opposed to what's *good enough*. We hunt for spurts of elation; chasing money instead of engagement and connection. Relationships foster long-term meaning; bring intrinsic value and, more importantly, happiness to the lives we live. The oddest thing is, we think of happiness as an achievement gained from our own doing.

The Ripple Effect

Worshiping autonomy exploits egoism and greed, when deeply embedded in us all is altruism and a need for transcendence. Self-proclaimed militant atheist Richard Dawkins believes in a *selfish gene*, that has us moving up the hierarchy of natural selection through more altruistic multi-level selection. Dawkins explains that similar to bees who give up their lives for the good of the hive, humans transcend from independent states of mind to thinking that is more inclusive.

Serving others however, serves us only through free will. If we derive our motivation from obligation, shame, or even pride, we don't receive the same satisfactory boost. Only when the recompense is intrinsic do actions and words increase our self-concept and sense of purpose. The evolution of an identity (as a representation of our unique human spirit) has emerged from society's collective mind—in other words, by comparison, we formulate a distinction, an identity. We're only as rich or poor, benevolent, or intelligent as our neighbor, or better said, our neighborhood. Moreover, each generation and socio-economic plane brings with it a new paradise to consider.

It's clear that a deeper understanding of humanity is at the bedrock of our psychic survival. The prehistoric hunt-gather-eat mindset has evolved to quick-witted processing of search-click-share. Yet, in our fast speed age, the notion of a collective mind hasn't gone viral. Consider that like our bodies and brains which have evolved for higher functions (brain's have grown a pound to make room for our prefrontal cortex) so too is the developing of our collective consciousness underway. There's a ripple effect to all of our choices impacting not only our own evolutionary process, but also that of others; this is our legacy, our life extended through the lives of others. Our moral virtues are after all, more useful to the collective than they are to the individual. Recognizing this oneness of our ability to adapt and survive together is transformative.

Waiting Game

I think of this extended life, as I once again sit in an oncologist lobby waiting for results. I've learned to appreciate the awkward waiting time in these reception areas –filled with unconditional love—believe it or not. Women who've never met before lean into one another, and share intimate stories of sickness and despair to provide comfort and companionship. Across the room, a mother wearing a head wrap sits next to her pristine teenage daughter who chatters excitedly about the brand new license she got to use to drive them there. Another man impatiently bounces his knee until his wife returns; quickly standing to embrace her as he listens for her results. A close friend calls these waiting rooms marriage counseling—I call it life counseling.

True equality exists in doctors' lobbies. Pain, sickness, love, and fear exist for us all, no matter who we are or what we have. Each time the medical door swings open, tension suspends in the air as all those in the room look up to see who will come out the door, or who they call in. My lobby companion is called in next and our words trip each other as we say, "Good Luck," instead of farewell. When you're sitting there you watch the parade of these new temporary friends enter and exit, trying to read their facial expressions, searching for a sign that they've received a clean bill of health. When you see smiles, you search for their eyes to congratulate them with your own. When you see tears, you look down with respect for their privacy, while praying that you may have more time to make the most out of your life and with the fear and insight that you may be the one needing the same type of privacy next when it's your turn to walk out that door.

These are places of limbo, where the world of hectic schedules and to-do's melt away, where the purpose in your life becomes crystal clear, connecting to that which you love, in meaningful ways, for as long as possible. Life is unpredictable, and uncertainty brings angst. According to *A Course in Miracles*, "Those who are certain of the outcome can afford to wait, and wait without anxiety." If we believe every outcome will ultimately serve us, then there's nothing to fear. Even if the future brings pain, when discomfort arrives, we no longer fear it, we come to know it and so we cope. Nevertheless, uncertainty unnerves us—it drives us crazy—and more often than not, we create all sorts of imaginary worst-case scenarios. Ruminating about what is the right choice, or what could go wrong, puts us on guard. Moreover, to be on guard is to be in fear.

Our mind is transformative and miraculous, capable of taking the seemingly impossible and inconceivable to overcome into a more magnificent transmutation of self. Eventually we all find a way to adjust. Even when our external world worsens, our consciousness heightens to a new plane of understanding. To elucidate the miracle that is our mind, consider the following study. Researchers followed a group of adults who had a 50/50 chance of inheriting the Huntington's gene—a disease that triggers irreparable nerve damage to the brain and a shorter life expectancy. Before undergoing genetic testing, participants took psychological evaluations to measure their well-being and depression rates. After given the results of the test, participants were surveyed across three time intervals: immediately after, in six months, and finally after one year. Not surprisingly, individuals who tested positive for the gene reported increased depression rates, but only initially. Half a year later, those who had received the devastating news they'd likely die in middle age reported having returned to their happiness baselines. Those who decided not to take the test or who had inconclusive results, on the other hand, were actually less happy a year later, even when compared to those who now knew they carried the incurable gene.

The happiness set point theory suggests there is a place of equilibrium we inevitably adjust to after the highs and lows of life. We fear sickness, poverty, and pain but time is a great healer and although we may go through times, which are hard to endure, faith (free will to believe in the unseen) centers us in knowing we're never alone and there's an intrinsic benefit to each experience. Upon returning to our baselines, we can cross the threshold to post-traumatic growth that can raise our happiness set point. Human beings are resilient; we come to terms with the events of our lives by applying purpose and meaning. Tal Ben-Shahar Ph.D. names those who see the opportunity inside challenges as Benefit Finders. As we find ourselves in the sinkhole of despair, we mount our ladder to climb out. Each rung acts like a thought. Finding significance inside despair, however small the benefit may be—one positive thought to the next positive—helps us climb out of the sinkhole of sadness to peak through the full splendor of new light.

Paradigm Shift

In her book *The Vortex*, Esther Hicks compares our thought process to a playground spin wheel. For our thoughts to gain momentum and move in a positive direction (without tremendous effort), we have to jump on the spin wheel when it is moving slowly. Forty percent of our daily actions aren't actual decisions, but habits – automated effortless reactions performed without thought. In addition, most of our inner chatter is also habitual. In the wise words of Yongey Mingyur Rinpoche, "Ultimately, happiness comes down to choosing between the discomfort of becoming aware of your mental afflictions and the discomfort of being controlled by them." Start by asserting a truth that feels real (no matter how small or insignificant it may seem). This will allow you to reach for the next positive thought to gain momentum, until eventually, you're inside a spin wheel of positive thinking, living out joy with seemingly little effort.

Changing decades of learning isn't easy when our environment reminds us repeatedly that our happiness quotient depends on the amount of choices that money, status, and health can afford us.

Nonetheless, the chain of habitual erroneous thinking can be broken through practice. Observing our internal dialogue slows down our spin wheel of thinking. Thoughts do not define who we are, rather it's what we chose to do with those thoughts – in action and course of thinking—that forms our character. Writing out more meaningful storylines fortifies happiness. In truth, we're constantly changing the landscape of our minds. Compare the mind to a forest, full of potential, but chaotic. It would be easy to disparage the land if there were no discernable paths. Each time we experience an event, we either create a new path (a new memory) or reinforce a former path (reinforce a memory). Each path leads us to a destination. Neural maps (or networks) are set for future ideas, memories, and expectations.

Scientists call this constant reshaping of our brains neuroplasticity. Neurons are the stepping-stones to our points of interest. The more stepping-stones or neurons laid on the path, the easier and quicker it is for us to walk across challenging terrain. Repeated action stabilizes the path converting a rudimentary trail to an automatic escalator.

Automation has us unconsciously step on our mind's conveyer belt that transports us to the most familiar paths. The easiest and most comfortable path isn't always the best. Sometimes these familiar habits, the fast and seemingly simplest to take, can be dangerous (such as giving into unhealthy cravings, addictions, or harmful relationships, just to name a few). The familiarity of these negative transit systems traps us into making the wrong choice regularly—limiting our growth potential.

Every system of thought must have a starting point. Conscientiousness can introduce roadblocks when needed. With time, these roadblocks allow the weeds and grass to grow around the neural walkways to make the path harder to traverse in the future. Instead, a new alternative route begins to form in its place, which often can be more beneficial.

It's pretty amazing to realize that some highly complex and sophisticated belief systems can be based on one initial thought and once the momentum builds, these systems link up and take on a life of their own. Patterns of thought create belief systems. So really listen to your thoughts! If the narrative is repetitive and counterproductive, change its direction. The way out is to choose one thought and examine it, and then let go of any others. A single paradigm shift can transform our way of thinking forever. For the most part, the brain works on intuition stored up from the memory of pain, pleasure, and interest. Instinctively, the brain tries to conserve energy, automating what it can, and prejudging the rest. However, beyond our genetic computation, is free will. How we choose to drive our thought patterns and behaviors ultimately determines our sense of purpose and well-being. According to Nobel Laureate and the father of Behavioral Economics, Daniel Kahneman, author of *Think, Fast, and Slow,* the brain has two modalities:

- (Fast) System 1 — energy efficient automated and reactive.
- (Slow) System 2 — focused attention, mindful decision-making processes.

If System 1 is the set point, the natural impulse and intuition center, then System 2 is moral conscience and self-awareness. Imagine if every interaction felt like a moral dilemma, it would be emotionally and mentally exhausting. Therefore, although habits can be helpful, if not examined properly, they can also lead to mental afflictions. Learning to habituate our patterns of behavior to reflect our core values can make our intuition and automated responses less effortful and more integrated to our higher order thinking (System 2-which we associate as holding our self-concept and identity).

That's why it's so critical to *mind the gap.*

The Space Between

Chasers often envy the perceived advantages of others, without considering the benefits of our privations. Even if the only benefit is perspective, a deeper insight into what we treasure allows us to appreciate what we already have. Then, we can choose what we're willing to sacrifice and what we're not.

My father grew up riding horses and watching sunsets on a small island made of an inactive volcano (3 miles in diameter) off the coast of Honduras. Banana boats are the main form of transit between the mainland and the island. In the short ride between the hustle and bustle of the real world into this small paradise of green, a thick layer of musky air envelopes the skin in a protective layer to buff off the stress of daily life. As the salty bits of the ocean jump up to kiss your lips, even the Internet feels like a need of the distant past, a laughable concept. The grace of nature is profound.

The minute you disembark, school-age children greet the boat— begging to be chosen to help lift up bags. Young boys with the strength of men lift fifty-pound suitcases upon their over-developed shoulder blades in one full swoop. The heavy weight of responsibility they carry humble American parents who worry about the weightiness of their kids' school book-bags. While riding through the bumpy roads of the small town, in the back of a twenty-year-old pick-up truck, a beautiful yellow clay cathedral appears behind a public market. The items sold in that market are to satisfy basic necessities—no designer clothes or fancy iPads.

My father, a local celebrity, is the Americanized village boy personified. As he jumps off the truck the eyes of the town's people draw closer, they look at him as Americans contemplate the Kardashians. Conversely, we observe the islanders like the National Geographic. Two biospheres appear so far apart from one another; the natives romanticizing luxury, Americans romanticizing simplicity. There aren't any high-rise hotels, let alone universities there. Those seeking more opportunities, like my father, must leave for higher education elsewhere.

My Abuela (Grandmother) Meches instilled in my father a deep appreciation of his roots, reminding him always to remember where he came from, but also to recognize where he was meant to go. Now he returns to lay his mother to rest in Amapala's (Honduras) volcanic ground. A formidable line gathered around her casket as practically the whole village paid their respect around this teacher and humanist who always gave what little she had to those who needed it more. Her involvement in the Red Cross helped so many that listening to the townspeople retell stories of her charity and altruism extended her influence past her last breath.

On the day of my departure from the island, my father and I walked hand and hand down the peer to say our goodbyes. Standing at the peer's end, his arms around me, we watched the sunrise. The birds celebrated the arrival of the sun emerging out of the dark water, and a double bound rainbow showed itself off. Instinctively my father took out the camera and began taking pictures. Here we stood—father and daughter, both bona fide workaholics—moving around, shooting from various angles trying to make the scene more productive when all we really needed to do was take it in. He moves me into frame and like a whiny little girl, I said, "Can we take a picture with our soul, Papa?" Laughing at the child-like tone and spirit—we both knew what I meant: Let's not remember our time together with pictures, let's memorialize inside us; allow nature to adjust the rhythm of our energy, if only for that moment. Routinely in an effort to capture the moment we lose it, looking to Facebook for the captured moments we didn't live.

That island's most valuable resource is perspective. In our search for meaning, if we're lucky, we find the place where inner-peace resides. Like the boat ride from the mainland to the island, leaving behind the hassle of the have-to's and to-do's to be present in the moment, engages inner awareness. Nevertheless, we need the appropriate navigational tool to circumnavigate the waters of daily life to get us to the right destination—where we actually want to go. Constructing principles that reflect what is most important to us, makes us the topographers that illustrate the most scenic views of our most coveted paths.

Light of Intention

The truth is, we get stuck in the details instead of enjoying the big picture. Discontentment becomes our captain when we disengage with the simple things in life, which can give us unaltered, unencumbered joy. The illuminating lighthouse of consciousness can guide us home through intention. Having a clear understanding of our intentions (despite actions or outcome) helps us stand confidently in our authenticity.

The *Intention of the Day* is a single phrase I write out every morning as a reminder to stay connected to the present moment, rather than letting my mind wander to what would be better than now... the melancholic days of yesterday, or the promises of tomorrow. This word changes every day, although there are favorites like *breathe, savor,* or *listen,* which often find themselves on the real estate of my wrist. Like tiny billboards, they're in my constant line of vision, prompting me to connect to the Oneness of all things. To act with intention is to act with purpose in mind, a mental goal to align a value to the day.

Intentions give us permission to stop apologizing to others, or ourselves for the mistakes we make. Since thoughts have the power to affect our days, having clear intentions takes control of our happiness. Ritualizing *Morning Intentions* into our home has had a profound affect on the way we, as a family, think, act, and feel when we meet with challenges. At the beginning of our morning, each one of us sets an intention and by the days end we talk about how that value challenged and rewarded us throughout the day. These small nudges to mindfulness are tools that teach our children not *what* to think, but *how* to think—how to hardwire their own happiness.

"I See You"

Subjective happiness stems from our self-concept and sense of purpose, whereas purpose is derived from how significant we determine our lives to be. As we learned earlier in this chapter, studies have shown that if we serve a purpose outside ourselves—create a sense of altruism—we can adjust our happiness set points upward. Marrying intention to a daily practice has us find meaning in small things. For example, if my intention of the day is to let go when I disappoint someone by asserting my truth that may be in contradiction to someone else's opinion, instead of feeling guilty or angry, I let go. I refrain from judgment and further rhetoric. Instead I allow myself to stand my ground and give the other person the right to have a difference of perception without attaching my self-concept to their opinion of me. I let go of being a people pleaser, and allow myself the right to be me.

The day is full of energy boosters and drains. I'm constantly trying to un-hurry myself in order to bring positive energy into the room and not suck it dry. We sense this exchange of energy when we describe people as draining or motivating. Referring to those individuals who help me, or whom I help serve, by name—be it a customer, waiter, grocer, etc.—along with a sincere act of kindness, helps slow me down. This practice instantly engages my senses. Using people's names, is a reminder we're here to help one another, not just fill a role, or job description. I've heard the argument *it's their job*. Yes, this may be true but each one of us chooses how we will serve.

In fact, the tone of an entire day can change when strangers become friendly acquaintances. A jovial tone or a smile aren't just good manners, they're small gestures of unconditional respect. Poet Maya Angelou once said, "I've learned that people will forget what you said, people will forget what you did, but people will never forget how you made them feel." So many people come in and out of our days and, sadly, we snap out requests, with our eyes focused on smart phones, menus, etc. To our detriment, we fail to acknowledge that who stands before us is a *person*, not a robot. Instead of engaging with others through everyday activities, we devalue our exchange – and turn interactions into transactions. The milk, the eggs, the cereal are scanned in the grocery line. The cashier says, "Was your experience pleasant?" without looking up. Checking off the grocery list, a "Great, thanks" is automatically exchanged much like the credit card being processed. We part ways without once looking into each other's eyes. Off we go, onto the next sterile interaction, to cross off more of the long to do list of the day, the week, months, and years. This habit of getting things done quickly and efficiently may be productive in a single day, but it's counterproductive to finding deeper engagement in the course of our lifetime. When we convince ourselves there's not enough time to slow down, we discredit the value of each singular moment. Two simple words—thank you – can change a thought, feeling, or situation in a heartbeat. When someone has chosen to show up to help – in any capacity— remember to share appreciation. It's amazing how the energy shifts for both the giver and the receiver.

Knowing and acting according to commandments, moral codes, and righteousness, though, is not the same as breathing life into them. Saying hello to a stranger with a smile, a word of appreciation, or coupling of someone's hand in a handshake—all are small gestures of unconditional respect. Not one of these gestures takes more than a few seconds, but they exercise our human connection. We can arrange playdate activities, take the laundry to the drycleaners, buy dinner, but to be fully present, the work and the to-do's need to leave our minds, if only for the moments when another human being is in front us. When we're able to relate with people across professions, situations, and boundaries, we pay homage not only to the individual but also to humanity itself.

Fighting for the Prize

The boxer, like rebellion of Chasers, has been rewarded with heavy gold title belts. Their victory speeches preach, "Work hard, and then harder, be a fighter" Ra, ra, ra, applause, applause. We worship fighters like demigods. Then we're surprised when we prizefight our way to our own defeat. We're all messengers of truth, cautionary tales, and role models, simultaneously. We're enough as we are, but not good enough to stand in the podium of perfection. Finding peace rests in accepting our humanness and experiencing the grace of a Higher

Power. Yet, we protest it. Spirituality isn't weakness; it's our inner-humanity reaching out for interconnection. When we sense that force within us, a sense of belonging arises, even if it offends our ego's need for grandiosity. You can't intellectualize spirituality. We over think what a *Higher Power* is, instead of recognizing that it is humanity's evolutionary force embedded deep within us to guide an inner wisdom.

Though we fight it, our most meaningful relationship *is* with a Higher Power—whatever name or label it may hold. It's unfortunate, but we are stuck in semantics. Words like *spiritual* get auto-corrected to *woo-woo* and religious morphs into judgmental. There are moral codes and modes of conduct for each that our identities play ring-around-the-Rosie around. The spirit of life's game is lost when we compete with principled virtues. Like the game of box-ball where one big box is divided into four, each religious box tries to beat out its opponents by throwing dogmatic curve balls into competing courts.

Out of the illusion, is the trinity of Oneness—the interdependency of ourselves, humanity, and a Higher Power. Call your G-d what you will, call this G-d your Higher Self if you're more comfortable with a name that is not aligned with an institution, but listen to the prayer you hold closest to your heart. The engagement in this relationship with your Higher Self ultimately determines how your consciousness will choose to interpret the events of your life. There's no way around it. It's the difference between getting on a hedonic conveyer belt, or climbing the evolutionary ladder to inner peace. Now that's a prize worth fighting for. Rabbi Hillel, one of the most influential scholars in Jewish history, offered this poetic prayer:

If I am not for myself who will be?

If I am only for myself what am I?

If not now, when?

CHAPTER 12

Mommy CEO

"From two individuals, one life is conceived yet born from the womb of a single woman—from our Oneness—we develop and separate. This is the delicate dance of Life moving to a spiritual rhythm."

- Solange Jazayeri

*W*hen I held my daughter for the first time, I lost myself in love. The feeling was so powerful I was instantly willing to give away all of me to her. I thought motherhood required us to let go of anything that got in the way of the greater good of the family, which includes (but is not limited to) career, time, and selfishness. Loving our little babies makes sacrificing our identities an easy decision. Living with that decision, however, is immeasurably hard.

It was hard for me to separate where my ambition ended and where my fears began. Hard work was the rock that stabilized and tethered me to the ground. However, when I sold my business I could no longer rely on production to validate who I was. You can work all day in the home, only to look back and feel like nothing was accomplished. In fact, being productive in the home is having a house look like it was not lived in all day.

Moving from businesswoman to full time stay-at-home mom felt strange and uncomfortable. Without a measuring stick of financial goals and accomplishments, I felt unstable. I was so afraid of being ordinary and average, that I failed to appreciate how an ordinary day can come alive. Sweeping the floor and washing the dishes are not necessarily creative activities; they can feel seemingly mundane and ordinary. Nevertheless, witnessing my grandmother, Mama Dora, do these same acts with love and care for our family each day has humbled me to a new perspective. It is not what you do, but with what level of care and purpose, you do something that matters. I am an enigma to my Spanish grandmother. In a very candid conversation between us, she asked why I worked so hard when the life afforded to me by my husband meant there wasn't a need to do so. Wasn't I happy with what was around me? We are extremely close, so the Gringa in me wanted to shout out, "Are you kidding me!?" Respectfully I refrained, listening to her advice instead. She went on to say there's no need to search outside our home and ourselves when the simple things in life can give us exactly what we need. House chores can bring contentment if we see the bigger picture. We don't have to own a business or have fancy titles to feel productive and important. Focusing our attention on the value of our contribution is what brings purpose and meaning.

Keeping the house clean and organized gives our families a sense of comfort and security. After a long day of work, Nick looks forward to walking into a home that feels warm and inviting. Remembering the days where I worked overtime I, too, badly wanted to come home to a happy home and a happy wife. Our homes are our own piece of the universe. It is the place where we feel the safest and most loved, where we allow ourselves to just *be*. On the days my husband comes home to an upside-down chaotic mess, the sense of peace on his face cannot be found. Inside our homes lives the spirit of our family. Mondays are my favorite days to clean up. They are messy mornings and a trail of weekend happenings. Each toy that is picked up and each gadget that is out of place revives the weekend's memories of all of us just *being* together.

Finding an identity outside the home brings me closer to my full potentiality, but my grandmother had a point. Her plea was that we find contentment with what lives within us, not by seeking happiness outside of ourselves. The achievements we accomplish are special moments in our life. For so long, I thought I was a certain kind of person— the kind of person who didn't waste her time away with meditating. Instead, I spent my time multi-tasking. Perhaps that is why I found myself so lost when I decided to stay home and devote myself to my family entirely. Hiding under a cloak of personal achievement no longer served who I was now. Feeling inadequate in my new role as a mother, I tried to gain my footing again with the best way I knew how: bridging business leadership and communication to the home. After all, CEOs and mothers share the same responsibilities: teaching and inspiring the team to reach their full potential.

I took on the challenge with the same vigor and enthusiasm I had in the early days of my career. Like a novice trying to prove myself to a demanding boss, I became a mother octopus, juggling eight things at once. Whatever activity I was engaged in at the moment, guilt for not taking care of some other activity of equal importance invaded my consciousness. I read countless books and began tackling the home as if it were a business in need of high performance and high efficiency. Each day had activities to pep me up for the daily duties: Mealtime Mondays, Two-load Tuesdays, and Wipe-down Wednesdays...,etc... Although these rules of engagement apply at work, at home the productivity model of being 100 places at once doesn't apply. Our families want our full presence. To automate our life with habits that focus solely on getting things done and getting things in order, can have us using valuable resources of time and energy that can be better spent engaging with one another.

The habit-forming exercise you will find in the Teaching Tools section was first used to teach my daughter French. I thought this would be a great gift. Every time we drove to and from school, we could increase our foreign language vocabulary together. What fun it would be! Ok, it was fun at the beginning when breakfast began with chocolate croissants and when we bought cool Parisian bonnets, but after a couple of weeks, I missed my little girl telling me what had just happened at school. Of course, I still wanted to give her more advantages in her future but not at the cost of our conversations in those moments inside the car where there were no added distractions to steal her attention away from our bonding. Although giving up the Mini Cooper for a minivan-like car and changing the entrepreneur title for that of chauffeur took some time to get used to, in all those car rides to school, to ballet practice, to playdates, and birthday parties, I've had some of the most meaningful tête-à-têtes to date with her. French car lessons can wait—there is Google translate now.

Many of the systems in the teaching section of this book have been taken from business, communication, and leadership theories. The need for a more engaged team is a universal need for us all, both in our work lives and our home lives. However, keep in mind that our family culture is different from one we would find at work. Our morning schedule has rituals, not tasks. Rituals are used to heighten our sense of togetherness and that helps us all to run out the door inspired, not harried, and crazed. By setting a standard in our home of agreements, codes of behavior, and a unified vision, we are better at focusing our efforts on what connects us best to each other, and most of all, to our authentic self.

At times, this means sacrificing our likes and desires for the good of the family. At other times, it means holding one another accountable for our actions. Inspiring our families with fun activities and rituals is easy; it is the facilitating their growth through consequences and endless homework that is the tough part. Parents need grit too. To help raise our children, we need to commit to a philosophy and system that works best for our own distinct family.

Begin Again

Let me depict for you a day in the life of the Jazayeris: I am breathing. Inhaling in, exhaling out. Slowly my emotions reign in as Isadora leaps from one couch to the next. As she takes these leaps of faith our toddler below her looks up. In my mind's eye, I can see a jump falling short and Isadora trampling over her sister Nazareen, catching Isadora's fall like the safety mats in a gymnastic studio.

I'd leave the chaos of this room if I could, but Nick has rested his hand on my leg while he watches TV, arresting me to this couch. After a long week of work and our two conflicting schedules, I know he wants to be near me, so I balance the computer on my right knee while his hand rests on the left. Completely oblivious to my need for concentration, the noise of the room gets louder. The giggles compete against laughter, and laughter soon begins to compete with the increasing volume of the TV's surround sound. It's best I close the computer and either go to another room or choose to be completely engaged in this one. Instead I continue to balance family and work, like the balancing act of my computer and my marriage on either side of me. I calmly but tersely plead, "I'm trying to concentrate, please quiet down." I'm negotiating with my family—but more with myself. It's Saturday. I want to spend time with them, but I also want to hit a deadline. At a gridlock, I sit here impatiently, quietly trying to be a good wife, an okay mom, and a crappy businesswoman. Therefore, I resolve to appreciate my husband's affection and correct my sub-par work later. Then I will play dolls with the girls and make up for the lack of enthusiasm I had at their trampoline-like moves.

But how can you concentrate when there is a circus ring around? Just breathe. One more time, breathe. I begin typing again. Can't Nick see I am trying to concentrate? He is old enough to understand. How would he feel if the girls were jumping up and down on his dental chair as he tried to perform a root canal?

Passive-aggressively, each time the girls jump, I let out yet another deep sigh, while they beam in their dismount. The frustration rises, but still, I continue to breathe... deeper and deeper. I'm getting sick of breathing. Now, Nazareen screams and yanks a toy away from Isadora. Like the lady at the circus slowly pushing the fire stick down her throat until it **shoots** back like a dragon, I furiously shout; "Fudge! Enough! PLEASE BE QUIET!" (I didn't really say fudge).

Man, that felt good! Like the momentary relief of ears finally popping at 10,000 ft. in the air. Suddenly the hazy noise becomes clear and crisp and I hear my voice and thoughts more clearly. All those years of meditation, deep breathing, and mind over matter control—down the tubes! But damn, that felt good. Just as my gaze settles on my family's doe eyes staring back at me, I feel horrible. That momentary relief of taking off the heavy backpack of resentment was now gone and now I'm picking up the heaping load of guilt. There is a pause as they wait for my next move. With the knot of guilt still in my throat, I let it out, "I'm sorry. I lost it. I am so sorry, I screamed... and cursed." Since I came from a stereotypically passionate Latin family of loud screams and warm embraces I had promised myself that when I grew up, I'd keep the yummy hugs and get rid of the intense screaming. As a pacifist, watching myself explode onto the people I love the most in this world was an indication I had crossed the line from stress into crazyville.

I looked at Nick, waiting for him to say something accusatory. Isadora, however, spoke first, "Mom, I know that wasn't you, I know that was just your brain." Nick followed her statement with, "Just go to the other room. You don't have to yell or use that language. It's okay. We get it... don't feel bad. Just do what you have to." Instead of making me feel inadequate, he points to the reason of my outburst, intuitively understanding that the reason why I am doing this balancing act (which is obviously not working) is that I love them. They went back to their activities without missing a beat, continuing as if they didn't experience a crazy fire-breathing lady.

I walked to the other room broken-hearted. However, before I start to beat myself up, I hear Isadora's words repeat themselves inside my head, "I know it's not you mom". She speaks over those Reservoir Cats that were waiting for their invitation to come in and hold space. Isadora and I have a practice that whenever we feel anxious or angry, we question whether we have an opened mind or a closed brain. In this case, it was obviously a very closed brain. Rather than opening my mind to myriad better choices, my brain had exploded with frustration. As I sat with my thoughts, I realized that although my screaming was disappointing and far removed from conscious parenting, I can't be that bad if my five-year-old daughter can explain the difference between our brain's frustrated reaction and our true inner nature. If my daughter can give me permission to be a human being, then I can do the same for myself. "Purposely engage in acceptance and kindness," I say aloud as I walk myself back into the room, accepting that I can't do it all and do it well.

Radical Acceptance

Central to the theme of unconditional love is self-acceptance and acceptance of others. If our goal is to share our being with those around us, we must accept we are not what we do but who we are. One common question women tend to ask is "When is there time to focus on me when everybody around needs me?" The answer is simple but hard to embrace. To emit unconditional love, you must first accept what you and others are capable and incapable of doing. In addition, do this without judgment. Focus your attention on activities that exercise your values: choose your television programming wisely, get involved in your tribe's gatherings, share kindness by looking at everyone you speak to in the eye.

Cooperation over autonomy brings about connection and intimacy. When we are able to figure out what we're capable or incapable of being, then we are better able to attract people in, drawing deeper connections with them. Let's stop judging ourselves against ideals and start focusing on the value of relationships. Communicating our limitations and our boundaries may mean having the tough talks and letting the tension and disappointment rise, but honest dialogue protects individuals and allows for personal growth and understanding inside a relationship. Telling your boss at work you can't work overtime because you have family obligations or communicating to your girlfriend you feel uncomfortable with her gossiping are tough yet necessary talks.

By first being clear and compassionate with ourselves and then with others, we honor our inner being. At times honoring the energy of our being means protecting it from feeling drained. The best way to prevent energy drain is to know when it is appropriate to say *yes* and when to say *no*. It's okay to have personal boundaries. When our only value is marked solely on others' happiness and satisfaction, we jeopardize a deeper connection with our own being. Asserting what is right for us may be hard because it can bring about disappointment. We may not be able to do as many activities as we would like, or have as many possessions as we desire, or even please as many people as we wish to. However, in exchange, we are able to have more of what we value and need when we say *no* to things that drain our spirit and we say *yes* to that which fulfills us. Compassion is the practice of accepting our limitations with kindness. Accepting we are enough despite our limits is the true meaning of unconditional self-love.

Ancestral Archetypes

Like bronze statues, our cast is molded from that of the last. A child is born and his or her features are instantly auctioned off. "S/he has his eyelashes, grandma's temper, my hair..." and the list goes on until the poor infant is left with nothing to claim as his or her own. I've been culpable of this: taking credit for what's good, blaming my husband for the challenges, and referring to the zodiac or extended family for the unexplained. Our view of the world and the view we have of ourselves are in large parts determined by our family's culture.

I come from a long line of Type E* women. My great-grandmother, Mama Yaya, lived to age ninety-four. She was a kind, hard-working businesswoman with a convenience store in a small island in Honduras. Traveling to New Orleans to buy merchandise wasn't common, but it proved to be a successful strategy for her and with it she proved more industrious than most women of her era did. Industrious, cultured, and independent, at a time and in a place where divorce was heavily frowned upon (and virtually unheard of) she took control of her home, finances, and three children and divorced a man she could no longer depend on to help the well-being of their family.

Alone, she took care of her children emotionally and financially, always securing sufficient life insurance and life lessons so they could take care of themselves if the need ever came.

Despite her Catholic upbringing, self-respect overrode an unfulfilling, failing marriage. A doctrine was created by my great-grandmother, the matriarch of our family: self-sufficiency breeds liberation. Her archetype is one that generations of women in our lineage have followed. (We pass on more than simple biology; we pass on little bits of our soul... and little bits of our struggles as well.) Her daughter, my grandmother Mama Dora, also divorced, and she too, worked hard to be self-sufficient and not only provide her children with security, shelter, and love, but an advanced education here in the United States.

Their independence was courageous and noteworthy—so the message to be self-reliant took root. Then it sprouted, and like the game of telephone, each generation passed on the message in a slightly different manner. By the time I heard it, my interpretation was I could only depend on myself and should therefore be as independent as possible – in every area of my life – but particularly in regards to the opposite sex.

I was born romantic and tenderhearted—different from stout I thought—and so this, I interpreted as weakness. Frailty was not an option. To protect my soul I hid my delicate nature. Instead of letting myself be known, I tried to squeeze inside the archetype of a strong independent woman. However, as we've discussed, archetypes are just illusions. At some point, we realize we'll never be enough or have enough if we allow fantasies to define who we are and what we need. Somewhere along the way, I learned the lesson she intended for me to receive, that what truly liberates us is not self-sufficiency, but self-respect.

It wasn't until becoming a mother that I went back to interpret the story of their lives for what they truly had been. The reputation of these two great women is a legacy of self-respect, not staunchness, or wealth. My great-grandmother worked side-by-side with her children, giving kindness to their customers, finding ways to make everyday conveniences affordable for the poor. More than a little neighborhood store it was a community center. Mama Yaya's legacy lives on past her life, because what she gave to her children was given to their children. That gift of kindness and self-respect is larger than any monetary inheritance (and it lasts much, much longer).

For The Next Generation

"Dio a luz!" in my mother's native tongue means to give birth and is translated to mean *to give light*. Our duty as human beings is to bring light into the world. It is in our eyes that others search for their purpose and meaning. People want desperately for us to acknowledge, admire, and love them because it is in loving others that we grow to understand love, which, in turn, leads to learning to love ourselves. We are mirrors to one another, projecting our fears and admiration outward.

When others light up upon our arrival, we feel as though our existence is confirmed. But, in our search for validation we find ourselves giving parts of ourselves away to fit the expectations of who we *should become* and who we *should be*. Doing so makes us lose hold of who we are, lose sight of the inner light that is exclusively ours.

We give ourselves to others because it allows us to experience the love within us. Loving too much is not the risk, nor is failing to love ourselves enough the problem. Distrust is what we contest; not having enough faith that our Authentic Self will lead us to rewarding relationships and inner peace. Our **Reservoir Cats** are distrusting because they try to protect us from hurt and pain (a.k.a. embarrassment of the Ego). They tell us we only have our self to rely on, but when we get out of our head and into our hearts, we come to recognize we are all in this together. **"Hurt people, hurt people"** is perhaps a simple cliché, but powerful nonetheless. The pain others parlay unto you is their pain, not yours.

One day we will have to leave our children. If I could choose only one thing to leave behind, may it be that they accept the miracle of their soul for who they are, love this miracle unconditionally, and defend it against all costs, sharing it with one another. With **their self-acceptance,** I know they will be all right. May they find peace and courage to go after their full potentiality as they live brilliantly and authentically in this world.

Mommy CEO

In 2010, Mommy CEO was founded to help women fulfill their potential by learning to listen to their authentic voice. Women inspire evolutionary change. This movement to look inward develops our inner being, our families, our communities, and ultimately the world.

Our philosophy:

Within us lies all that is needed to live fulfilling lives as wives, mothers, and women, encouraging the next generation to move onwards.

Maybe: Within us lies all that is needed to live fulfilling lives as wives, mothers, sisters, and women and the love needed to encourage the next generation to evolve to higher places of integrity, compassion, and strength.

This book has been influenced by the philosophies, methodologies, and measurable applications we practice at Mommy CEO. The theories and practices are a product of extensive research on communication, and leadership, as well as the qualitative research by leading behavioral and humanistic psychologists, and biological anthropologist Helen Fisher. Also of great influence to this book was Dr. Harriet Braiker, who was the first to illuminate the Type E* woman's dilemma.

Happiness is not only a feeling—it's a choice, not always the easy choice, but a choice nonetheless. Developing young minds redefines paradigms. How easily we understand the unconditional love and respect children deserve. However, we too are like these little human beings, each of us in process, learning and growing – at different paces, of course – but moving ahead. In addition, our choices today, create the future of tomorrow. Without language or title, children remind us where we came from and where we are going. Their "Why, Why, Why?" examines our "what." What philosophies and ways of living do we choose to embed in them?

Epilogue

Thank you. From the bottom of my heart, I thank you. We are all incredibly busy and yet you took the time to carve out some space for the reading of this book.

Every Monday, Isadora's school asked parents to write a short note to remind our children how loved and special they are. I took this as an opportunity to share my lessons learned, hoping to instill in her that the best things in life are the ones we enjoy in the present and not chasing the future.

These praise notes became a seed that bloomed inside our relationship. Each story opened conversation and insight, as much for her as for myself. At a time when I did not have a business nor a project to call my own, these letters to my daughter took a life of their own. The best way to learn is to teach. Therefore, I began reading and researching how to hardwire happiness into our everyday life so I could teach my daughters how to hold on to their authentic self as they grow.

The more I read the more I wanted to share. Soon enough the conversations with those around me began to take form. Truth be told, the kindness of complete strangers suggesting that I write a book motivated me to put the knowledge I had acquired on paper.

What first began as a passion project soon became a labor of love. It wasn't always easy to face myself, to be honest and candid. There were chapters where I rested my coffee cup beside my wine glass.

The research was both insightful and heart wrenching at times. There were chapters that felt like a confession and others that felt like purgatory. *It's Just Business* in particular had me realize how little I knew about politics. How I had stood behind the phrases "I'm not a feminist" or "I'm not into politics" as an excuse to remain ignorant and without responsibility. Now looking at the statistics, I know it is not enough to complain. Women make 85% of all purchasing decisions in our country. We are voting with our dollars each and every day. We must also stand up in our own way and let our voices be heard so our families may enjoy a better tomorrow.

Many of us are waiting for the voice of G-d to awaken us from the deep slumber of mindlessness to be directed to a life's calling. As westerners, we think this requires hard work and effort. I respectfully disagree. Hard work and effort test our commitment to excellence (be it as teachers, scientists, and/or mothers) and as we walk into positions of leadership (be it as managers, entrepreneurs, or civic activists) we are the ones shaping the mindset of our culture's future.

We all have the ability to reach for sustained happiness by letting go of our constant need for more and accept who we are. Appreciating our *being* more than *doing,* can change our internal states of mind but it begins from communicating from within and learning to consolidate all the identities that comprise who we are.

Empowerment and liberation are not at the top of the mountain but at the base of it. To take the first step towards inner peace, we must first empower and liberate ourselves. In the past decade of my life, my focus has shifted from what I want to achieve in life to what I want to leave behind, not achievements but a legacy. Today, I understand it is not about pursuing something outside of our grasp. Rather than enjoy the view from the top, I want to enjoy the climb, develop courage, resilience, and growth.

If the top never comes, let's at least enjoy the journey of getting there, slowing down to appreciate the scenery of each new altitude. Each stage is harder than the last, but much more beautiful and rewarding.

To remain in conversation and receive more detailed information and exercises, please join our community online.

Resources

Chapter 1:

1. Opening Quote

Multi-millionaire Sidney Harman from A Whole New Mind: Why Right-Brainers Will Rule the Future by Daniel H. Pink

Validated Self-esteem vs. Self-respect

2. Carol Dweck, Phd. and Claudia Mueller 6 Studies:

https://www.stanford.edu/dept/psychology/cgi-bin/drupalm/system/files/Intelligence%20Praise%20Can%20Undermine%20Motivation%20and%20Performance.pdf

3. New York Times Bestseller, Paul Tough, author of *How Children Succeed*

Evolving Together

4. Bell Curve

https://lesacreduprintemps19.files.wordpress.com/2012/11/the-bell-curve.pdf

5. (Carnegie Information) New York Times Bestseller, Paul Tough, author of *How Children Succeed*

Roman's Story

6. Tal Ben-Shar's 2004 thesis: *Restoring Self-esteem's Self-Esteem: Constructs of Dependent and Competence and Worth*

The Value of Time and Money

7. Mihaly Csikszentmihalyi, Finding Flow: The Psychology Of

Engagement With Everyday Life

Seeking Validation in External Measures

8. The Bhagavad-Gita

9. Helen Fisher, Phd. Why Him? Why Her?

Chapter 2:

Beginning quote. The Power of You!: How YOU Can Create Happiness, Balance, and WealthHardcover – August 11, 2006 by Scott Martineau

The Third Parent

10. Pat Mitchell Quote from documentary Miss Representation. Therepresenattionproject.org/fils/miss-representation/

Born Pretty

Science and Media

An Evolutionary Function

'Fun'draising

11. The relationship between women's genital self-image and female sexual function: A national survey Laura Berman, Mieke Ana Windecker http://link.springer.com/article/10.1007/s11930-008-0035-4#page-1

12. Michael P. Goodman, MD. Female Genital Cosmetic and Plastic Surgery: A Reviewjsm_2254. http://www.drmichaelgoodman.com/wp-content/uploads/2011/05/Article_JSM_2011_FGPS_Review-first-one.pdf

13. The American College of Obstretricians and Gynecologists issued warning I 2007 ACOG Committee Opinion No. 378: Vaginal "rejuvenation" and cosmetic vaginal procedures. http://www.ncbi.nlm.nih.gov/pubmed/17766626

14. 53,332 vaginal rejuvenation surgeries are performed in the United

States, representing a 50 percent increase from 2008, according to an estimate from the **American Academy of Cosmetic Surgeries** http://www.cosmeticsurgery.org/

"Strike A Pose...Vogue, Vogue, Vogue"

15. Eckhart, Tolle quote book New Earth

16. 1948, Alfred Kinsey http://www.kinseyinstitute.org/research/ak-hhscale.html

Accepting Our Vulnerability

17. Naomi Wolfe, book Vagina

18. Thompson, Sonya. "Study Shows 1 in 3 Boys Heavy Porn Users". University of Alberta Study, 5 March 2007

Completely Exposed

Our Bodies, Ourselves...the Next Stage

Namaste Little Bunny

19. Brown University http://www.brown.edu/Student_Services/Health_Services/Health_Education/nutrition_&_eating_concerns/body_image.php

20. Jenna Jameson book How to Make Love Like a Porn Star: A Cautionary Tale

Chapter 4:

21. Erika Harris quote: The POWER of Your Intense Fragility: What culture hasn't told you about being sensitive AND strong.

Front and Center

22. The Paradox of Declining Female Happiness

http://users.nber.org/~jwolfers/papers/WomensHappiness.pdf

23. Citi and LinkedIn survey http://www.forbes.com/sites/shenegotiates/2012/10/09/third-of-career-women-dont-include-marriage-children-in-definition-of-success/

24. Women breadwinners.
http://www.nytimes.com/2013/05/30/business/economy/women-as-family-breadwinner-on-the-rise-study-says.html?_r=0

25. Special Report produced exclusively for The Wall Street Journal Executive Task Force for Women In The Economy 2011 Unlocking the full potential of women in the U.S. economy

26. Breadwinner moms http://www.pewsocialtrends.org/2013/05/29/breadwinner-moms/

27. MIT & Carnegie Mellon University, and Union College study. Putting Heads Together. New Study: Groups Demonstrate Distinctive 'Collective Intelligence' When Facing Difficult Tasks. http://mitsloan.mit.edu/newsroom/2010-malone2.php

28. "Overcoming the Backlash Effect: Self?Monitoring and Women's Promotions," Olivia A. O'Neill and Charles A. O'Reilly III, Journal of Occupational and Organizational Psychology, 2011.

29. ENGAGEMENT AT WORK: ITS EFFECT ON PERFORMANCE CONTINUES IN TOUGH ECONOMIC TIMES KEY FINDINGS FROM GALLUP'S Q12 META-ANALYSIS OF 1.4 MILLION EMPLOYEES. http://www.gallup.com/strategicconsulting/161459/engagement-work-effect-performance-continues-tough-economic-times.aspx

Code of Silence

30. You Just Don't Understand: Women and Men in Conversation Paperback – February 6, 2007 by Deborah Tannen

Side by Side

31. Christina Hoff debate at http://intelligencesquaredus.org/debates transcript: http://intelligencesquaredus.org/images/debates/past/transcripts/men-are-finished.pdf

32. WHEN EVERYTHING CHANGED by Gail Collins. Michelle Obama quote http://www.whitehouse.gov/the-press-office/remarks-first-lady-a-corporate-voices-working-families-event

Baby Elephant in the Room

33. Family Act or the Family and Medical Insurance Leave Act. https://beta.congress.gov/bill/113th-congress/house-bill/3712. http://www.nationalpartnership.org/research-library/work-family/paid-leave/family-act-fact-sheet.pdf

Chapter 5:

Cat Fighting

34. Daring Greatly: How the Courage to Be Vulnerable Transforms the Way We Live, Love, Parent, and Lead Hardcover – September 11, 2012 by Brene Brown (Author)

The Faces of Eve

35. Effect Of Colors: Blue Boosts Creativity, While Red Enhances Attention To Detail. http://www.sciencedaily.com/releases/2009/02/090205142143.htm

36. The Farther Reaches of Human Nature Paperback – October 1, 1993 by Abraham H. Maslow (Author), Bertha G. Maslow (Preface), Henry Geiger (Introduction)

Stepping Into Shoes

37. Mindset: The New Psychology of Success Paperback – December 26, 2007

by Carol Dweck (Author)

Those Type of People

38. The Millennials: Connecting to America's Largest Generation

Hardcover – January 1, 2011

by Thom S. Rainer (Author), Jess Rainer (Author)

Chapter 6:

39. Multiple Intelligences: New Horizons in Theory and Practice Paperback – July 4, 2006 by Howard E. Gardner (Author)

Pretty or Smart?

40. Beauty Pays:

Why Attractive People Are More Successful

Daniel S. Hamermesh

41. Leaner Prion sentences http://www.economist.com/node/21526782

42. The Strength of the Halo Effect in Physical Attractiveness Research

43. http://www.dailymail.co.uk/sciencetech/article-1347651/Attractive-people-higher-IQs-Beauty-brains-DO-together.html

http://en.metapedia.org/wiki/Race_and_physical_attractiveness

Intelligence and physical attractiveness. Satoshi Kanazawa. Department of Management, London School of Economics and Political Science, United Kingdom

http://personal.lse.ac.uk/kanazawa/pdfs/i2011.pdf

You Eyeballing Me?

44. Mindfulness (A Merloyd Lawrence Book) Paperback – January 22, 1990

by Ellen J. Langer

45. Why Him? Why Her?: How to Find and Keep Lasting Love Paperback – January 5, 2010 by Helen Fisher (Author)

Impostor Syndrome

46. The Secret Thoughts of Successful Women: Why Capable People

Suffer from the Impostor Syndrome and How to Thrive in Spite of It Hardcover – October 25, 2011

by Valerie Young (Author)

47. L'eggo My Ego: Reducing the Gender Gap in Math by Unlinking the Self from Performance

Shen Zhang, Toni Schmader, and William M. Hall

http://www.ncbi.nlm.nih.gov/pmc/articles/PMC3821772/

An Altered Mind

Chapter 7:

48. Swami J (Swami Jnaneshvara Bharati) http://www.swamij.com/reflections.htm

49. The Type E* Woman: How to Overcome the Stress of Being Everything to Everybody Paperback – April 21, 2002

by Harriet Braiker (Author)

Symphony No. 5
Where did the Romance go?
Super Women

50. The Type E* Woman: How to Overcome the Stress of Being Everything to Everybody Paperback – April 21, 2002

by Harriet Braiker (Author)

Chapter 8

Size Matters

51. http://www.cnn.com/2006/WORLD/europe/09/13/spain.models/

52. http://www.bbc.com/news/magazine-17453822

Changing The Standard

53. http://www.change.org/p/abercrombie-fitch-ceo-mike-jeffries-stop-telling-teens-they-aren-t-beautiful-make-clothes-for-teens-of-all-sizes

Victoria's "Secret"

54. International Positive Psychology Association (IPPA)

First World Congress on Positive Psychology

55. Barbara L. Fredrickson http://incubator.rockefeller.edu/?p=1949

http://www.positiveemotions.org

56. Martin, J. B. (2010). The Development of Ideal Body Image Perceptions in the United States.Nutrition Today,45(3), 98-100. Retrieved from nursingcenter.com/pdf.asp?AID=1023485

https://www.nationaleatingdisorders.org/get-facts-eating-disorders

57. Professor William Whitehead. Phone interview cited in https://www.lagrangerx.com/library.php?id=644320

http://www.pointofreturn.com/gut_health.html

58. Gianrico Farrugia. http://www.elle.com/beauty/health-fitness/emotional-eating-the-brain-stomach-connection-445031

59. http://www.jamieoliver.com/us/foundation/jamies-food-revolution/home

Getting off the Treadmill

60. Dr. Neff http://www.self-compassion.org

Chapter 9:

Vulnerability and Intimacy

Feeling Connected

Embracing Our Differences

61. Framingham http://www.health.harvard.edu/newsletters/Harvard_Mens_Health_Watch/2010/July/marriage-and-mens-health

Healthy Dependence
Evolving Together

62. Nielsen, L. (2007, March 1). College daughters' relationships with their fathers: A 15 year study. *College Student Journal, 41*(1), 112-121. Retrieved January 29, 2009, from ERIC database

63. Fatherless homes. *What Can the Federal Government Do To Decrease Crime and Revitalize Communities?* from the National Institute of Justice, 1998, page 11 https://www.ncjrs.gov/pdffiles/172210.pdf

Out of Darkness

Chapter 10:

Sum of its Parts

64. The National Longitudinal Survey of Adolescent Health, Musick and Meier http://www.human.cornell.edu/pam/outreach/upload/Family-Mealtimes-2.pdf

Accepting the Truth
She Said, He Said
We Belong Together

65. Kelly McGonigal. http://www.ted.com/talks/kelly_mcgonigal_how_to_make_stress_your_friend

Rebuilding Trust
Divide and Conquer
Women Warriors
The Final Frontier

66. Mother Theresa http://www.scu.edu/ethics/architects-of-peace/Teresa/essay.html

67. Dalai Lama at the 2009 Vancouver Peace Summit https://www.youtube.com/watch?feature=player_embedded&v=Tic2ups2n78

Chapter 11:

68. http://sonjalyubomirsky.com

69. A measure of subjective happiness: Preliminary reliability and construct val...

Lyubomirsky, Sonja; Lepper, Heidi S

Social Indicators Research; Feb 1999; 46, 2; ABI/INFORM Global pg. 137

http://sonjalyubomirsky.com/wp-content/themes/sonjalyubomirsky/papers/LL1999.pdf

The End of the Rainbow

70. Study by University of British Columbia and Harvard Business School http://dunn.psych.ubc.ca/files/2010/11/From-Wealth-to-Well-Being-Money-Matters-but-Less-Than-People-Think-2009-Updated-June-2012.pdf

Ripple Effect

71. The Selfish Gene: 30th Anniversary Edition—with a new Introduction by the Author Paperback – Deluxe Edition, May 25, 2006

by Richard Dawkins

Waiting Game

72. A Course In Miracles Paperback – May 21, 2008

by Foundation For Inner Peace

73. Hutington's study. The psychological consequences of predictive testing for Huntington's disease. Canadian Collaborative Study of Predictive Testing.

Wiggins S1, Whyte P, Huggins M, Adam S, Theilmann J, Bloch M, Sheps SB, Schechter MT, Hayden MR.

http://www.ncbi.nlm.nih.gov/pubmed/1406858

74. Tal Ben-Shahar http://www.talbenshahar.com

Paradigm Shift

75. The Vortex: Where the Law of Attraction Assembles All Cooperative Relationships Paperback – August 12, 2009

by Esther Hicks

76. The Joy of Living: Unlocking the Secret and Science of Happiness

by Yongey Mingyur, Daniel Goleman

77. Thinking, Fast and Slow Paperback – April 2, 2013

by Daniel Kahneman

78. http://mayaangelou.com

Fighting for the Prize

79. Rabbi Hillel Quote first read in The Exquisite Risk: Daring to Live an Authentic Life

by Mark Nepo

Beginning Quote for end of Chapter Summaries

80. (derived from a series of studies published in 2009, Nike Foundation. (2009) The Girl Effect: Not Just about Girls: Engaging Men and Boys is Key to Girls' Ability to Achieve their Full Potential [Internet]. www.nikefoundation.com/media_room.html [Accessed 19 May 2009]